Introduction

Food Finder

C000061350

INTRODUCTION

Time for Food guides are designed to help you find interesting and enjoyable places to eat in the world's main tourist destinations. Each guide divides the destination into eight areas. Each area has a map, followed by a selection of the restaurants, cafés, bars, pubs and food markets in that area. The aim is to cover the whole spectrum of food establishments, from gourmet temples to humble cafés, plus good food shops or delicatessens where you can buy picnic ingredients or food to cook yourself.

If you are looking for a particular restaurant, regardless of its location, or a particular type of cuisine, you can turn to the Food Finder, starting on page 4. This lists all the establishments reviewed in this guide by name (in alphabetical order) and then by cuisine type. Note: many Hong Kong restaurants are in tower blocks or in hotels.

PRICES
Unlike some guides, we have not wasted space telling you how bad a restaurant is – bad or poor value restaurants simply do not make it into the guide. Many other guides ask restaurants to pay for their entries, or expect the restaurant to advertise in return for a listing. We do neither of these things: the restaurants and cafés featured here simply represent a selection of places that the authors have sampled and enjoyed.

If there is one consistent criterion for inclusion in the guide, it is good value. Good value does not, of course,

▲ Man Wah

necessarily mean cheap. Food lovers know the difference between a restaurant where the high prices are fully justified by the quality of the ingredients and the excellence of the cooking and presentation of the food, and meretricious establishments where high prices are merely the result of pretentious attitudes.

Some of the restaurants featured here are undeniably expensive if you consume caviar and champagne, but even haute cuisine establishments offer set-price menus (especially at lunchtime) allowing budget diners to enjoy dishes created by top chefs and every bit as good as those on the regular menu. At the same time, some of the eating places listed here might not make it into more conventional food guides, because they are relatively humble cafés or takeaways. Some are deliberately oriented towards tourists, but there is nothing wrong in that: what some guides dismiss as 'tourist traps' may be deservedly popular for providing choice and good value. Establishments which have the approval of the Hong Kong Tourist Association advertise the fact by displaying a small red junk logo.

FEEDBACK

You may or may not agree with the authors' choice – in either case we would like to know about your experiences. Any feedback you give us and any recommendations you make will be followed up, so that you can look forward to seeing your restaurant suggestions in print in the next edition.

Feedback forms have been included at the back of the book and you can e-mail us with comments by writing to: *timeforfood@thomascook.com*. Let us know what you like or do not like about the restaurants featured here. Tell us if you discover shops, pubs, cafés, bars, restaurants or markets that you think should go in the guide. No food guide can keep pace with the changing restaurant scene, as chefs

▲ Tin Hau Temple

move on, establishments open or close, and menus, opening hours or credit card details change. Let us know if you discover changes – say to telephone numbers or opening times.

Symbols used in this guide

VISA	Visa accepted
⓭	Diners Club accepted
MasterCard	MasterCard accepted
🍴	Restaurant
🍷	Bar, café or pub
🧺	Shop, market or picnic site
∅	Telephone
◉	Transport
❷	Numbered red circles relate to the maps at the start of the section

The price indications used in this guide have the following meanings:

⑤	budget level
⑤⑤	typical/average for the destination
⑤⑤⑤	up-market

FOOD FINDER

▲ Hanging poultry

Hong Kong Island: Central and Soho districts

Central – the very hub of Hong Kong's economy – offers a myriad of top-quality restaurants and its luxurious hotels are used heavily by the business community. A newly trendy area, Soho (South of Hollywood Road) has come alive following the construction of a 750m-long pedestrian escalator leading up to Mid-levels from Central Market, and its abundant bars and eateries now rival those of Lan Kwai Fong.

HONG KONG ISLAND: CENTRAL AND SOHO DISTRICTS
Restaurants

The Bayou ❶

9–13 Shelley St, Soho

✆ 2526 2118

◉ Pedestrian escalator from Central Market

Open: daily 1200–1430, 1830–2230

Reservations recommended

All credit cards accepted

Cajun

❷❺

A slice of sun-washed Louisiana with generous helpings of authentic Cajun and Creole dishes (jambalaya, fried green tomatoes, ribs, praline sweet potato pie). The Bayou Bar next door (even more laid back and great for watching passers-by on the escalator) serves tasty snacks, overfilled sandwiches and oysters all day. True Southern hospitality.

Blue ❷

G/F 43 Lyndhurst Terrace, Soho

✆ 2815 4005

◉ Pedestrian escalator from Central Market

Open: Mon–Fri 1200–1300, 1930–2230, Sat–Sun 1930–2230

Reservations essential

All credit cards accepted

Jacket required

Fusion

❸❺❺

Sophisticated dining in a cool, steely-blue interior, where intriguing east–west combinations are presented with style.

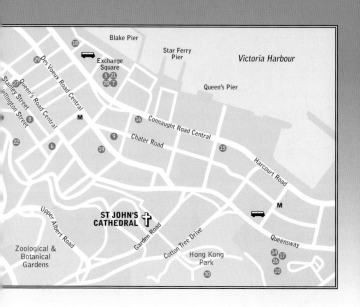

Blake Pier

Star Ferry
Pier

Victoria Harbour

Queen's Pier

18

29 Des Voeux Road Central

Exchange
Square

5 21
28 7

21 Queen's Road Central

Stanley Street

Wellington Street

8

22

M

6

16

9

19

Connaught Road Central

Chater Road

15

Harcourt Road

M

Upper Albert Road

ST JOHN'S
CATHEDRAL ✝

Garden Road

Cotton Tree Drive

Queensway

14 17
26
10

Zoological &
Botanical
Gardens

Hong Kong
Park

30

▲ Hong Kong Island

▲ Luk Yu Tea House

The two floors ooze simplicity and understated elegance; you really feel like taking your time over lovingly prepared dishes. Portions are generous, tasty and as spicy hot as you want them to be. As well as Thai favourites (*tom yum* soup, green and red curries) the chefs have borrowed a little here and there from neighbouring Burma such as honey-glazed savoury banana fritters!

Hunan Garden

3/F The Forum, Exchange Sq., Central

✆ 2868 2880

Ⓜ MTR (Central/Hong Kong Station)

Open: daily 1130–1500, 1730–2400

Reservations recommended

All credit cards accepted

Hunan

⑤⑤

Serving what some consider to be one of the best regional Chinese cuisines, the spacious Hunan Garden excels: the minced chicken soup in bamboo and stuffed boneless chicken (which must be ordered in advance) are specialities. Like Szechuan, Hunan food can be hot and spicy, and the fried chicken with chilli is a fine example! Live folk

Try the coconut prawns with banana and Asian caramel ... and don't miss out the stunning desserts. Anyone who's anyone dines here.

Café au Lac ③

G/F 20 Staunton St, Soho

✆ 2526 8889

Ⓜ Pedestrian escalator from Central Market

Open: daily 1200–1500, 1800–2400

Reservations recommended

All credit cards accepted

Vietnamese

⑤⑤

An ideal introduction to the subtleties of North Vietnamese cuisine. Café Au Lac serves a helpful mixed starter, wonderful whole fish, pancakes stuffed with prawns, fried soft-shell crabs and tender *satay* beef in a clay pot. Tiny tables are set quite close together, and the service is charming. Cosy.

Café Siam

40–2 Lyndhurst Terrace, Soho

✆ 2851 4803

Ⓜ Pedestrian escalator from Central Market

Open: daily 1145–1430, Mon–Fri 1800–2300, Sat–Sun 1800–2400

music is laid on in the evenings. Airy.

Jimmy's Kitchen 6

Basement, South China Buildings, 1–3 Wyndham St, Central

☎ 2526 5293

🚇 MTR (Central)

Open: daily 1130–1500, 1800–2300

Reservations recommended

All credit cards accepted

International

❸❸❸

No guide could possibly omit Jimmy's. Opened in 1928, its eclectic menu is perhaps short on surprises but long on quality and reliability. The seafood mixed grill and chicken Kiev are old favourites, as are Jimmy's own oriental dishes and the baked Alaska dessert. Comfortable yet stylish, Jimmy's has the feel of an old China club, with attentive staff who care a great deal. An institution.

Joyce Café 7

The Atrium, 1 Exchange Sq., Central

☎ 2810 0807

🚇 MTR (Central), Star Ferry Hong Kong

Open: Mon–Sat 1200–1500 and 1900–2330

Reservations recommended

All credit cards accepted

International

❸❸

The emphasis is on light, healthy gourmet cooking with lots of vegetables and fish; red meat is a recent addition to the menu. Designers and shoppers stop off here for fresh juice and a light lobster lunch … or devilish desserts. There are sister cafés at: *1/F The Galleria, 9 Queen's Rd, and 4/F Prestige Tower, 23 Nathan Rd.*

Luk Yu Tea House 8

24–6 Stanley St, Central

☎ 2523 1970

🚇 MTR (Central)

Open: daily 0700–2200, *dim sum* 0700–1800

Reservations essential

No credit cards accepted

Cantonese

❸

Service is brusque (if not gruff), but this is a must. The décor just post-dates the Second World War and the ceiling fans, high-backed booths, brass spittoons and art-deco stained-glass panels are classic and conservative. Most famous for its delicious and traditional *dim sum* and *yum cha* (where your steamed dumplings are served with an accompanying stock now seldom seen). Compulsory.

Peking Garden 9

B/1, Alexandra Hs, 16–20 Chater Rd, Central

☎ 2526 6456

🚇 MTR (Central)

Open: daily 1130–1500, 1730–2330

Reservations recommended

All credit cards accepted

洞庭樓

湖南菜

HUNAN GARDEN Restaurant

Peking
🌑🌑🌑

The Peking Garden thrives on theatre: there are extravagant noodle-making displays, ceremonies for breaking the clay around Beggars' chicken, and Peking Duck is served up with gusto. For showmanship it can't be beaten (and, unsurprisingly, it attracts a lot of tourists). This is one of 11 branches. Theatrical.

Petrus 🔟

56/F Island Shangri-La, Supreme Ct Rd, Admiralty

✆ 2820 8590

🚇 MTR (Admiralty)

Open: daily 1200–1500, 1830–2230, closed Sun lunch

Reservations recommended

All credit cards accepted

Jacket required

French

🌑🌑🌑

Lush and heavily velveted, Petrus has transformed food into art. The 'menu gourmand' is an excellent way to savour exquisite creations without breaking the bank, whether it's grilled *foie gras*, snow crab salad, pan-fried barramundi in sesame seed crust or spicy roast quail that takes your fancy. Opulent.

El Pomposo

4 Tun Wo Lane, Soho

✆ 2869 7679

🚇 Pedestrian escalator from Central Market

Open: daily 1230–1430, 1830–2230

Reservations recommended

All credit cards accepted

Spanish

🌑🌑

An unlikely, candlelit alley hides a delightful trio: a cosy Spanish baroque bar that you just don't want to leave, **El Pomposo** itself, with delectable *tapas* (the medley of seafood is sublime), and the (more expensive) **Pavilion** with tiny tables and Louis XIV high-backed chairs serving elegant French cuisine. Perfectly done.

2 Sardines

43 Elgin St, Soho

✆ 2973 6618

🚇 Pedestrian escalator from Central Market

Open: daily 1200–1500, 1800–2400

Reservations recommended

All credit cards accepted

French

🌑🌑

Simple, spacious and something of an oasis, this relative newcomer has fast earned an excellent reputation. With oriental overtones, the otherwise staunchly Mediterranean cuisine is resolutely tasty, with a range of dishes from (yes, grilled sardines) and warm goats' cheese, to saffron-flavoured seafood soup and *escargot*.

Soho Soho 🔟

G/F 9 Old Bailey St, Central

✆ 2147 2618

🚇 MTR (Central)

Open: Mon–Sat 1200–1430 and 1900–2230

Reservations recommended for lunch; reservations essential for dinner

All credit cards accepted

British

🌑🌑🌑

Traditional British dishes are given a modern and minimalist dash of innovation, typical of an emergent 'London' cuisine. Salmon fishcakes laid on spinach, calves' liver and bacon with caramelised onions, black pudding with apple ravioli, and proper British puddings complete with clotted cream. A rare beast.

Zen 🔟

LG 1, The Mall, Pacific Pl. Phase 1, 88 Queensway, Admiralty

✆ 2845 4555

🚇 MTR (Admiralty)

Open: Mon–Fri 1130–1530, Sat 1130–1630, Sun 1030–1530; daily 1800–2300

Reservations essential

All credit cards accepted

Cantonese

🌑🌑

Just as sleek, up-market and stylish as its London branches, with a strong reputation in Hong Kong for high-quality Cantonese cuisine. The deep-fried, boneless chicken wings stuffed with vegetables and mushrooms with lemon sauce are special indeed. Polished.

HONG KONG ISLAND: CENTRAL AND SOHO DISTRICTS
Bars, cafés and pubs

The Bull and Bear ⑮

G/F Hutchison House, 10 Harcourt Rd, Central

🚇 MTR (Central)

Open: Mon–Sat 0800–0200, Sun 1200–2400

All credit cards accepted

The first English pub to be, literally, imported to Hong Kong, this is still one of the most popular casual drinking spots in Central. Mock Tudor beams, all the right pumps behind the bar, and friendly staff make this an easy stop.

The Captain's Bar ⑯

G/F The Mandarin Oriental Hotel, 5 Connaught Rd, Central

🚇 MTR (Central)

Open: daily 1220–1500, 1700–2400

All credit cards accepted

Still popular after all these years. Captains of industry, Westerners and locals get together here for the evening or as a prelude to dinner upstairs at **Vong** or **Man Wah** (see page 17) – or that last cognac on the way home. A mellow, live band, and comfort all round.

Dan Ryan's Chicago Grill ⑰

114 Pacific Pl., 88 Queensway, Admiralty

🚇 MTR (Admiralty)

Open: Mon–Fri 1100–2400, Sat–Sun 0900–2400

All credit cards accepted

If you're craving a really good burger, steak or ribs, a hearty brunch (served 0900 until 1700), a yummy tuna melt, or just a

▲ Pacific Place

drink at the popular bar, this is the place. It gets busy in the evenings and weekends, and is children-friendly.

Eating Plus 18

Shop 1009, 1/F Southern International Finance Centre, 1 King St, Central

🌀 MTR (Central), Star Ferry Hong Kong

Open: Mon–Sat 0730–2200, Sun 0730–2030

All credit cards accepted

Impeccable and modern, health is the *modus vivandi* at this concept eatery. An extensive range of noodle dishes (including soup noodles), vegetable options and fresh juices are on offer, with busy harbour views as you dine. Monosodium glutamate is banished.

Fountainside 19

Shop G6–7, The Landmark, 16 Des Voeux Rd, Central

🌀 MTR (Central)

Open: Mon–Fri 0800–2100, Sat 0800–2030, Sun 1100–1930

All credit cards accepted

This stylish and visible brasserie in the heart of Central's up-market shopping area serves delicious and generous portions, and desserts that always get top marks. Always popular, you may have to wait for a table – but it's worth it – especially when the offices empty at lunchtimes.

The Globe 20

39 Hollywood Rd, Soho

🌀 Pedestrian escalator from Central Market

Open: Mon–Fri 0730–1430, Sat–Sun 1100–1300; daily 1930–0100

All credit cards accepted

An open English pub atmosphere, with wood-panelled walls, a good range of ales, well-populated bar stools, filling bar food and even a quiz night. Relaxed and friendly, a welcoming rendezvous.

Katsu Kichi 21

Shop 11–12, G/F The Forum, Exchange Sq., Central

🌀 MRT (Central)

Open: Mon–Sat 0700–2100, Sun 0900–1800

💳 💳 American Express

Given its central business district location, the self-service food in this unpretentious café is very good value. The *Gyoza* (wonton style dumplings), sushi, noodle and rice dishes are all inevitably popular; if you're there early try an authentic Tokyo-style breakfast.

The Red Rock 22

Basement, 57–9 Wyndham St, Central

🌀 MTR (Central)

Open: daily 1700–0200; last food orders 2330

All credit cards accepted

Usually heaving with late-night revellers and

party-goers. If you can fight your way through the crowd, the restaurant area serves good snacks from the grill.

Sherpa Himalayan Coffee Shop 23

11 Staunton St, Soho

🌀 Pedestrian escalator from Central Market

Open: daily 1100–1500, 1800–2300

All credit cards accepted

One of the strongest caffeine boosts around, and some excellent Nepali dishes (much more delicate and generally milder than northern Indian food). If the Sherpa wins you over to this aromatic and flavoursome cuisine, try the **Nepal Restaurant** directly opposite.

Staunton Wine Bar and Café 24

10–12 Staunton St, Soho

🌀 Pedestrian escalator from Central Market

Open: Mon–Fri 0900–2300, Sat–Sun 0800–2300

All credit cards accepted

Unbelievably popular. Hong Kong's expatriates enjoy the breezy, open-fronted wine bar on two floors – a great place to watch trendy Soho wander by. Stop for tea or coffee, just drinks, or a light meal.

HONG KONG ISLAND: CENTRAL AND SOHO DISTRICTS
Shops, markets and picnic sites

Shops

Bagel Factory 25

41 Elgin St, Soho

🚶 Pedestrian escalator from Central Market

Open: Tue–Sun 0800–1900

💳 ⓓ American Express

Arrive early for the best choice of generously filled bagels (or phone ahead if stocking up for a New Territories walk on ✆ 2951 0755).

Coo 26

LG/F Seibu, Pacific Pl., 88 Queensway, Admiralty

Ⓜ MTR (Admiralty)

Open: Sun–Wed 1030–2000, Thu–Sat 1030–2100

All credit cards accepted

A food hall to rival Harrods of London: an excellent wine shop (a Bordeaux cellar and lots of Japanese beers), fresh foods, essentials (including organic baby food) and luxuries.

CRC Department Store Ltd 27

Chiao Shang Bldg, 92–104 Queen's Rd, Central

Ⓜ MTR (Central)

Open: daily 1000–1900

💳

The food section has a good array of Chinese sweets (dried and salted plums, prunes, sesame crackers), Chinese rice wines, teas, dried mushrooms and seafoods, table linen, chopsticks and souvenirs.

Fauchon 28

Shop 3–5, G/F The Forum, Exchange Sq., Central

Ⓜ MTR (Central), Star Ferry Hong Kong

Open: Mon–Sat 0700–2100, Sun 0900–1800

💳 🏧 American Express

The few tables outside, guarded by a couple of bronze water buffalo, are ideal for munching delectable sandwiches and evil pastries. The delicatessen has an excellent *charcuterie* and cheese selection, as well as a good choice of wines.

Markets

Central Market 29

Junction of Queen Victoria St and Des Voeux Rd, Central

Ⓜ MTR (Central)

Open: daily 0700–1000, 1700–2000

In this new, somewhat prosaic location, a quick visit none the less provides the complete assault on the senses you would expect from a bustling, poultry, meat, fish and vegetable market.

Picnic sites

Hong Kong Park 30

Cotton Tree Dr. and Supreme Ct Rd, Central

🚋 Peak Tram (Central Station), MTR (Admiralty)

Open: daily 0700–2300; aviary: daily 0900–1700

A landscaped sanctuary, blending tropical forests, lakes and fountains, with a spectacular aviary of over 500 exotic and rare birds. There is a children's playground, as well as ample quiet spots to enjoy a serene calm in the heart of Hong Kong.

▲ *Bok choi*

Corporate dining

Dining to impress

For many of its six million-plus residents (and a good number of visitors) Hong Kong is simply about business: a frenetic, commercial and materialistic mecca, a shameless and dedicated homage to making money ... where food itself is a serious business, and where business deals are struck every day in its prestigious restaurants and hotels.

Since all of Hong Kong seems to eat out all the time anyway, and since so much top dining takes place in hotel restaurants, how does the business visitor select the right venue to convey the right message?

The **Grand Hyatt Hotel** (*1 Harbour Rd, Wanchai; ∅ 2588 1234; ◉ MTR (Wanchai)*) oozes opulence and class, and virtually all of its stylish restaurants and bars are good business venues.

▲ The Grand Hyatt Hotel

The **Champagne Bar** (*lobby level, The Grand Hyatt Hotel; open: daily 1700–0200; all credit cards accepted; no trainers or baseball caps*) is always busy with city business folk in the early evenings. Lunch or dinner at the **Kaetsu** Japanese restaurant (*Mezzanine, The Grand Hyatt Hotel; open: Mon–Sat 1200–1430, 1830–2200, Sun 1100–1500, 1830–2230; reservations essential; all credit cards accepted; ❸❸❸*) will mark you as not only a connoisseur of fabulous food, but as someone with no financial worries whatsoever! The Kaetsu is formal, sophisticated and seriously pricey yet completely exquisite. There are private rooms for up to 16 people (for a fee). Just as sophisticated is **Grissini** (*2/F The Grand Hyatt Hotel; open: Mon–Sat 1200–1430, 1830–2200, Sun 1100–1500, 1830–2230; reservations recommended; all credit cards accepted; ❸❸❸*); its fine, northern Italian cuisine is counterbalanced by an exemplary wine list, and panoramic views of the harbour.

Across the waters, **The Regent Hong Kong**'s famous **Lai Ching Heen Restaurant** (*see page 59*) sends an equally opulent message; many local residents rate this (along with the **Man Wah** – *see page 17*) as some of the best Chinese cooking in Hong Kong. If you're after a classic, formal and high-quality Chinese meal in stylish but discreet surroundings, then **The Peninsula** hotel's **Spring Moon** is just the answer (*1/F The Peninsula, Salisbury Rd, Tsim Sha Tsui; ✆ 2315 3160; Ⓜ MTR (Tsim Sha Tsui); open: daily 1130–1500, 1800–2300; reservations recommended; all credit cards accepted; private rooms and car valet available;* ❸❸❸). The traditional blackwood screens and grand staircase transport you to old Shanghai, and impeccable service accompanies fine Cantonese cooking. As the host, you could do worse than select a light fish meal of drunken prawns, and steamed garoupa and shark's fin, followed by the Spring Moon's famous chilled mango pudding.

Hong Kong's own tycoons and residents will lunch in the members-only **Hong Kong Club**, near the Furama Hotel, or perhaps in the relaxed atmosphere of the **FCC** – the Foreign Correspondents' Club in Ice House Street. If you, too, are intent on conveying an 'old China hand' impression, book a private function room at the **Fook Lam Moon** (*see page 29*), and arrange for a pre-ordered banquet, served by meticulous and respectful staff.

Central district on Hong Kong Island is the business hub, where several office buildings – and their restaurants – are connected by air-conditioned, elevated walkways … a godsend to office workers and captains of industry in the fierce humidity of Hong Kong's summer. And after all is said and done, it is in Central that the **Mandarin Oriental** (*5 Connaught Rd, Central; Ⓜ MTR (Central)*), one of Hong Kong's older hotels, still plays host to business clients best of all. For a truly sumptuous Cantonese feast (the lightly steamed crab claws with ginger and rice wine are utterly beguiling), the **Man Wah** sits sedate and dignified on the top floor of the hotel, its classical, gold-trimmed blackwood décor facing out across the business district towards the harbour (*25/F Mandarin Oriental Hotel; ✆ 2522 0111; open: daily 1200–1500, 1830–2300; reservations recommended; all credit cards accepted; jacket and tie;* ❸❸❸).

> … a frenetic, commercial and materialistic mecca … where food itself is a serious business …

Alongside the Man Wah, **Vong** (*25/F Mandarin Oriental Hotel; ✆ 2825 4028; reservations recommended; all credit cards accepted;* ❸❸❸) offers hallmark Thai-Vietnamese fusion in a less formal, modern, supremely stylish atmosphere; it is hugely popular with media, advertising and beautiful people.

The serious, undistracted business lunches, though, happen at the **Mandarin Grill** (*1/F Mandarin Oriental Hotel; ✆ 2522 0111; open: daily 1200–1500, 1830–2300; reservations recommended; all credit cards accepted;* ❸❸); the lighting is just subdued enough, and the tables spaciously placed enough, to give a feeling of complete privacy – oh, and the food is fantastic.

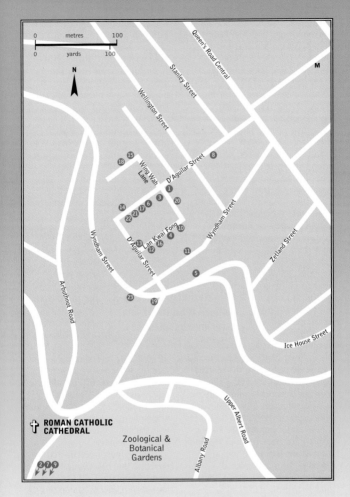

Hong Kong Island: Lan Kwai Fong and The Peak

The tiny streets around Lan Kwai Fong, originally full of flower markets, have been transformed into an eating and drinking mecca: after dark the streets fill with people, all looking to enjoy wonderful food and convivial evenings.

HONG KONG ISLAND: LAN KWAI FONG AND THE PEAK
Restaurants

Baci

2/F 1 Lan Kwai Fong

✆ 2801 5885

🚇 MTR (Central Exit D)

Open: Mon–Thu 1200–1430, 1900–2300, Fri–Sat 1200–1430, 1900–2330, Sun 1830–2230

Reservations recommended

All credit cards accepted

Italian

❸❸❸

Bright, almost stark and possibly the classiest pizza restaurant in Hong Kong with its crisp black-and-white décor. The pizza, too, is crisp and perfectly cooked. The menu offers no real surprises, but is guaranteed to deliver.

Café Deco

Level 1 and 2 Peak Galleria, 118 Peak Rd, The Peak

✆ 2849 5111

🚌 Bus 15 from Central terminal/Star Ferry pick-up; minibus from Star Ferry; Peak tram

Open: Sun–Thu 1000–2400, Fri–Sat 1000–0100; kitchen closed from 2300

Reservations essential

All credit cards accepted

Fusion

❸❸

The enormous and varied menu is bound to have something to tempt you. Café Deco (in the Peak Café group) has consistently won best restaurant awards. Oysters, sushi, pasta and grills are all prepared and served with flair, and the sheer decadence of the 1930s décor makes it a real treat. Generally good value and especially so if you opt for the set lunch. A stunning view (if you book early enough) caps off a perfect meal. Stylish.

Café des Artistes ❸

G/F California Tower, 30–2 D'Aguilar St, Lan Kwai Fong

✆ 2526 3880

🚇 MTR (Central Exit D)

Open: Mon–Thu 1200–1500, 1900–2230, Fri–Sat 1200–1500, 1900–1300, Sun 1900–2230

Reservations recommended

All credit cards accepted

French

❸❸❸

The windows on two sides make this bright and breezy and a delightful place to watch the world go by. The wooden floor and cane chairs create a casual feel – although it has a three-star menu. The southern French cuisine is of a consistently high

▲ Lan Kwai Fong

quality: the shallot and onion soup with thyme, Emmenthal and *etorki* gratin, and the rack of lamb in a pinenut crust with oven-dried tomatoes and fresh tarragon sauce are sublime. Provençal.

China Lan Kwai Fong

17–22 Lan Kwai Fong

✆ 2536 0968

⊛ MTR (Central Exit D)

Open: daily 1200–1430, 1900–2300

Reservations recommended

All credit cards accepted

Chinese

💰💰💰

All of China seems to be represented here, in a classic, up-market restaurant where the atmosphere is special, the waiters wear suits, the décor is formal traditional blackwood, and the food is exquisite. Try the wok-fried beef with black pepper in a potato basket. Dining here in 'The Fong', the prices are inevitably a bit high, but the atmosphere is fabulous. Impressive.

Indochine 1929 ③

2/F California Tower, 30–2 D'Aguilar St, Lan Kwai Fong

✆ 2869 7399

⊛ MTR (Central Exit D)

Open: daily 1200–1430, 1830–2300

Reservations recommended

All credit cards accepted

Vietnamese

💰💰

This charming, French colonial retreat offers the whole gamut of Vietnamese cooking; grilled shrimp on sugar cane, and soft-shell crab are well known – but try the baked pumpkin rice with chicken, shrimps and vegetables, and the roasted baby back ribs with lemongrass and spicy peanut sauce. Portions are generous and, as ever, it's best to plan on sharing.

M at the Fringe ⑤

1/F South Block, 2 Lower Albert Rd, Central

✆ 2877 4000

⊛ MTR (Central)

Open: Mon–Fri 1200–1430, Sun–Thu 1900–2200 and till 2230 Sat–Sun

Reservations recommended

All credit cards accepted

Mediterranean

💰💰

Michelle's has fast established a reputation for creativity, flair, attention to detail and marvellous presentation; the (hand-written) menu is beautifully balanced and ever-changing, and an evening in this trendy, colour-washed slice of old Italy is always a treat. Try the *tajines* and couscous, the soft-shell crab, and Mediterranean vegetable and goats' cheese terrine. A winning touch.

Il Mercato

34–6 D'Aguilar St, Lan Kwai Fong

✆ 2868 3068

Ⓜ MTR (Central Exit D)

Open: Mon–Thu 1130–2230, Fri–Sat 1130–2330, Sun 1700–2230

Reservations recommended

All credit cards accepted

Italian

$$

A friendly basement restaurant which is everything you'd expect of a family Italian restaurant. From *tricolore* salad and pizza, to pasta *quattro formaggi*, the dishes are all hearty and lunch is particularly good value. This place has a strong local following.

Mövenpick Marché Restaurant ⑦

The Peak Tower, Level 6 and 7, 128 Peak Rd, The Peak

✆ 2849 2000

Ⓜ Bus 15 from Central terminal/Star Ferry pick-up; minibus from Star Ferry; Peak tram

Open: daily 0900–2300

Reservations recommended

All credit cards accepted

International

$$

Mix and match from a self-service display of fresh, tasty and abundant Asian and European dishes. Enjoy one of Hong Kong's most stunning views at this ideal family destination (complete with children's playroom). For large appetites, the not cheap but never-ending buffet is well worth it.

Ning Po Residents Association ⑧

4/F Yip Fung Bldg, 10 D'Aguilar St, Central

✆ 2523 0648

Ⓜ MTR (Central Exit D)

Open: daily 1200–1445, 1800–2245

Reservations recommended

💳 💳

Shanghai

$

Hiding in an unlikely looking office building, this highly regarded restaurant has staunch local support. The drunken chicken (marinated in rice wine sauce) is superb, and for vegetarians, the tofu and the mock goose are exquisitely done. The staff are welcoming and attentive and, in spite of its Lan Kwai Fong location, this remains resolutely un-Westernised. A treasure.

The Peak Café ⑨

121 Peak Rd, The Peak

✆ 2849 7868

Ⓜ Bus 15 from Central terminal/Star Ferry pick-up; minibus from Star Ferry; Peak tram

Open: daily 1030–2400; kitchen closed from 2245

Reservations recommended

All credit cards accepted

Fusion

$$

▲ The Peak Café

A welcoming, reaffirm-
ing neo-colonial retreat;
spicy aromas greet you
from the open kitchen
with ceiling fans turning
lazily overhead. Try the
Indian-spiced tomato,
ginger and coriander
soup, or the wonderfully
refreshing seafood glass
noodles in a lime, chilli
and lemongrass dress-
ing, or go for a grill
from the impressive bar-
becue. Terrace tables are
coveted.

Post 97 🔟

1/F 9 Lan Kwai Fong,
Central

✆ 2810 9333

Ⓜ MTR (Central Exit D1)

Open: Mon–Fri 1000–0200,
Sat–Sun 24 hours

Reservations recommended
on Fri and Sat

All credit cards accepted

International

❸❺

Satisfying dishes – the
best thing about Post 97
is its all-night menu.
Relaxing – it has been
around for years, and
found its niche among
a mainly Western clien-
tele. Reliable.

Super Star Seafood Restaurant 🔟

19–27 Wyndham St, Central

✆ 2525 9238

Ⓜ MTR (Central)

Open: daily 1030–2400

Reservations recommended

All credit cards accepted

Cantonese-Chinese-Seafood

❺

One in a popular
restaurant group

(branches in Tsim Sha
Tsui, Harbour City and
Wanchai), specialising
in innovative *dim sum*,
where chefs revel in
new dumpling creations.
Go on a weekend for
the complete *yum cha*
experience and order
direct from trolleys, or
try a traditional basin
meal (*see page 87*) in
one of the most
decorated and plush-
verging-on-gaudy
venues in Central.

Thai Lemongrass 🄳

3/F California Tower, 30–2
Lan Kwai Fong

✆ 2905 1688

Ⓜ MTR (Central Exit D)

Open: daily 1200–1430,
1900–2300, closed Sun
lunch

Reservations recommended

All credit cards accepted

Thai

❷❸

The cooking is notice-
ably fresh and simple at
this tropical haven,
where Thai spices and
herbs are subtle and
complementary – not as
fiery as they can be.
The deep-fried *taro* and
prawn rolls wrapped in
fresh banana are a
perfect start, and the
bamboo fish with
tamarind sauce is a
must. An added bonus
is learning about Thai
food, as the menu is
categorised by region.

Tokio Joe 🔠

16 Lan Kwai Fong

✆ 2525 1889

Ⓜ MTR (Central Exit D)

Open: daily 1200–1430,
1830–2400; closed Sun
lunch

Reservations unnecessary

All credit cards accepted

Japanese

❸❸❺

A modern, slightly
pricey establishment
which none the less
serves delicate and
beautifully prepared
sushi and *sashimi*. The
special house sushi is
avocado wrapped
around deep fried soft-
shell crab, cucumber
and crab roe. Sushi with
an American accent.

Va Bene 🄳

58–62 D'Aguilar St, Lan
Kwai Fong

✆ 2845 5577

Ⓜ MTR (Central Exit D)

Open: Mon–Fri 1200–1430,
1900–2300, Sat 1900–
2400, Sun 1830–2300

Reservations essential

All credit cards accepted

No shorts

Italian

❷❸

For the robust, pure and
decisive dishes typical
of northern Italy this is
the place. Start with the
fresh artichokes sautéed
with olive oil and garlic,
and drool over the
morsels of pan-sautéed
garoupa wrapped in
thin-sliced courgettes
with pesto. The bread
basket is to die for.
Hong Kong's relatively
few Italians are huge
fans.

HONG KONG ISLAND: LAN KWAI FONG AND THE PEAK
Bars, cafés and pubs

Al's Diner and Bar 🔢14

27–39 D'Aguilar St, Lan Kwai Fong

Ⓜ MTR (Central Exit D)

Open: Mon–Thu 1130–0100, Fri–Sat 1200– 0300, Sun 1100–2400

All credit cards accepted

Complete with neon, stainless steel and high barstools, Al's is notoriously popular, especially late at night. Music gets louder as the night wears on. The diner menu runs to burgers, sandwiches and late/early breakfasts.

California 🔢3

30–2 D'Aguilar St, Lan Kwai Fong

Ⓜ MTR (Central Exit D)

Open: daily 1200–0200

All credit cards accepted

One of the early establishments in Lan Kwai Fong, and still famous for its cocktails and chic, American-style bar. The menu is good, with thick burgers and salads – but it tends to get too crowded on Fridays and Saturdays for comfort dining.

Club 64 🔢15

12–14 Wing Wah La., Lan Kwai Fong

Ⓜ MTR (Central Exit D)

Open: Mon–Sat 1100–2100

No credit cards accepted

The grass-roots feel at this unpretentious bar is in wonderful contrast to the rest of Lan Kwai Fong. Pre-1997, Club 64 was a popular rendezvous for student activists, and it still retains a slightly alternative but very relaxed feel. Friendly and welcoming, it has very long happy hours.

▲ Oscar's

NOODLE BOX

international jazz and blues musicians.

The Noodle Box 19

G/F 30–2 Wyndham St, Central

MTR (Central)

Open: Mon–Sat 1200–2300

No credit cards accepted

Run by the nearby **Wyndham Street Deli**, not only handy but serving immensely tasty noodles! Noodles with seafood, noodles with beef, noodles with vegetables, noodles with noodles! A quick (barstools and counter), hot and great value way to fill a gap.

La Dolce Vita 16

G/F 9–11 Lan Kwai Fong

MTR (Central Exit D)

Open: daily 1100–2400

All credit cards accepted

Another open-fronted bar, always packed with people-watchers, and a popular stop for many office workers on the way home. The Italian *antipasti* are highly recommended.

Insomnia 17

G/F Lee Comm Bldg, 38–44 D'Aguilar St

MTR (Central Exit D)

Open: daily 1700–2400 or later

All credit cards accepted

A godsend on a hot summer's night, with its open frontage and airy, neo-medieval church. Great for people-watching, with small tables at the rear, and good bar snacks.

Le Jardin 18

10 Wing Wah La., Lan Kwai Fong

MTR (Central Exit D)

Open: daily 1200–2400

American Express

A breezy, open-air terrace, upstairs at the end of the pedestrian lane, tends to attract a younger crowd. There is a small selection of oriental snacks.

The Jazz Club and Bar 3

2/F California Entertainment Bldg, 34–6 D'Aguilar St

MTR (Central Exit D)

Open: daily 2130–2400 or later

American Express

A great reputation for live jazz, with visiting

▲ View from The Peak

Oscar's 🔟

2 Lan Kwai Fong

🔘 MTR (Central Exit D)

Open: daily 1500–2400 or later

All credit cards accepted

For meeting friends, Oscar's is the 'in' place. Cool and up-market, the pavement outside is absolutely packed on a summer's evening.

Sherman's Bar and Restaurant 🔟

California Entertainment Bldg, 34–6 D'Aguilar St

🔘 MTR (Central Exit D)

Open: Mon–Thu 1200–0200, Fri–Sat 1200–0400, Sun 1700–0100

All credit cards accepted

Easy-going and relaxed, this is the sort of bar where, early on, one can actually hold a conversation. Live bands play on weekends. The *tapas* and salads are excellent.

Tribeca 🔟

38–44 Lan Kwai Fong

🔘 MTR (Central Exit D)

Open: Mon–Thu 1200–1500, 1800–0100, Fri–Sat 1200–1500, 1800–0400

💳 💳 American Express

Taking New York's Tribeca as its theme, the clean-cut American chic is pervasive. Staff are keen and the food is good, though not cheap.

Wyndham Street Deli 🔟

36 Wyndham St, Central

🔘 MTR (Central)

Open: Mon–Sat 0800–2100, Sun 0800–1800

All credit cards accepted

Wonderful sandwiches made to order, well worth the short climb up Wyndham Street. The friendly and attentive staff have an easy job tempting you into incredibly sinful cakes and puddings! Takeaway available.

Navigating Chinese cuisine

Geographical diversity

You are embarking on an adventure! Part of the gastronomic pleasure of Hong Kong lies in its different culinary shades and nuances ... and there are quite a few. China's 22 provinces cover over 9.5 million square kilometres, with climates as diverse as snow-topped mountains, desert plains and sub-tropical river basins. Unsurprisingly, therefore, China's 1.2 billion people enjoy a fairly wide culinary repertoire! To begin to understand its complexity, it is simplest to divide the country broadly into north, south, east and west.

Northern cooking is typified by **Peking** (Beijing) food, which is almost rustic, quite pure and basic – and very sustaining, as you would expect for the extreme cold temperatures of the north. The cooking is plain (roasting, baking or grilling), wheat flour breads are served instead of rice, and seasoning is quite minimal (although onions and garlic are plentiful). Peking food today is clearly influenced by that of **Mongolia**: 'hotpot' and Peking duck are typical examples.

Hotpot meals are big, communal affairs where tender mutton or beef, mushrooms and vegetables (especially cabbage) are added at the table. They not only keep the diners warm around the charcoal stove, but the stock just tastes better and better as the meal goes on. **Peking duck** (now so popular that Cantonese and other Chinese restaurants serve it too) has become world famous. The crispy, sweet, charcoal-roasted skin is eaten first, wrapped in paper-thin wheat pancakes with a little shredded spring onion, cucumber and sweet soya bean sauce; next move on to the succulent, tender duck meat, and finish with the light broth made with the duck carcass and vegetables.

Western Chinese cuisine is typified by that of **Szechuan** and its neighbouring province **Hunan**. The food is altogether more spicy and powerful, with rich, intense, palate-tingling flavours, and involves the copious use of ginger, sesame, aromatic peppers, garlic, onions, star anise, coriander and, of course, chillies,

▲ Peking duck

which are renowned for sweating out moisture in this generally humid climate. Cooking techniques tend to involve braising, crisp-frying or smoking, and many of the dishes are quite dry when served. Classics include **duck smoked with camphor-wood tea** (quite dry and very spicy, and perfectly complemented by yellow Shaoxing wine) and **twice-cooked pork**, which is sliced thinly, boiled, then crispy-fried and served with hot chilli and garlic chives. Fish dishes, of course, are few and far between.

One only has to consider the relatively opulent histories of **Shanghai**, **Suzhou**, **Nanjing** and **Hangzhou** to understand the rich **tastes of the East**, where wealthy dining inevitably involved great shows of imagination and complexity. Much of the cooking comprises stewing and braising (or red-braising, in rich, dark sauces), and significantly more sugar is used than in any other style of Chinese cooking. The emphasis is on crisp vegetables (often served separately) and supremely tender meats. Classic Shanghai dishes include **drunken chicken** (or prawns or crabs or pigeon) marinated in Shaoxing wine, **smoked fish** (actually not smoked but marinated in ginger, then fried and dipped in five spice) and succulent, freshwater eel and hairy crabs. Shanghai **vegetarian food** is equally creative. Vegetarianism was probably introduced with Buddhism in the Eastern Han period (AD 76–220), though since in some quarters it was deemed synonymous with poverty, many of the dishes were made to imitate meat.

Southern Cantonese food is most common in Hong Kong – and, for that matter, the Chinese cuisine most exported to Europe and America. It relies on good ingredients, good preparation (ingredients diced or shredded to the same size, in harmony with one another), light seasoning (sauces tend to be thin and clear), subtle flavours (hence its reputation for sophistication), variety (just look to the seafoods you never dreamed of eating) and brightly coloured, crispy vegetables. What is sometimes more difficult for Western palates to appreciate is the importance of texture; many foods are selected for texture alone, for example, **shark's fin** and **abalone**. A good stock is considered to be of supreme importance, and a basic mix of soy, Shaoxing wine, ginger, sugar and five spice can be replenished many times. Hot stir-frying is carried out with artful precision: timing is everything, and no single flavour is allowed to overshadow the others. Ultimately, a good dish will be judged for its clearness, blandness, texture and freshness. Indeed, for many, a fish, steamed simply with a little ginger, and moistened with a light stock and a few spring onions, is the very pinnacle of **Guangzhou cuisine**.

> ... the copious use of ginger, sesame, aromatic peppers, garlic, onions, star anise, coriander and, of course, chillies ...

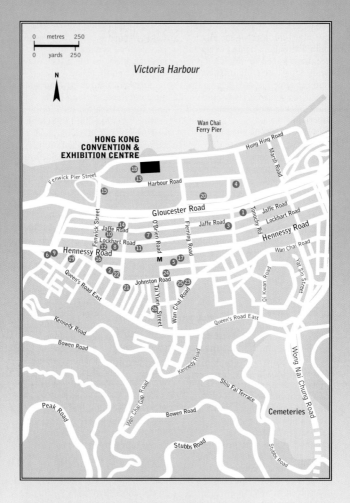

Hong Kong Island: Wanchai

Bar-city and home to the late-night reveller, Wanchai was formerly known for its tattoo parlours and red lights (and in fact is still a popular port-of-call for visiting naval fleets). Food-wise, however, frenetic Wanchai is one of the best places to find long-established local restaurants, with wonderful food at great value prices.

HONG KONG ISLAND: WANCHAI
Restaurants

Carrianna Chiu Chow Restaurant ❶

1/F 151 Gloucester Rd, Wanchai

✆ 2511 1282

🚇 MTR (Wanchai)

Open: daily 1100–2400

Reservations recommended

All credit cards accepted

Chiu Chow

💲💲

An old favourite, always packed and happily noisy, especially at lunchtime. Get into the swing by asking the waiter to choose for you (the English menu is limited) ... but be sure to have the special Chiu Chow roast goose and any of the other classic Chiu Chow dishes (often quite hearty and full of flavour). The *taro*-filled spring rolls are nectar.

Fook Lam Moon ❷

35 Johnston Rd, Wanchai

✆ 2866 0633

🚇 MTR (Wanchai Exit B2)

Open: daily 1030–2300

Reservations recommended

All credit cards accepted

Cantonese

💲💲💲

This branch enjoys a well-deserved reputation as one of Hong Kong's top Cantonese restaurants. The shark's fin and bird's nest soups come at scary prices, but seafood, pigeon and other dishes are much more manageable, and are all prepared to exemplary standards. Spread over several floors, you are escorted to your table with ruthless efficiency by a welcoming relay-team equipped with walkie-talkies!

Lao Ching Hing ❸

238 Jaffe Rd, Wanchai

✆ 2598 6080

🚇 MTR (Wanchai)

Open: daily 1100–2300

Reservations unnecessary

All credit cards accepted

Shanghai

💲💲

Hiding in the basement of the **Century Hong**

▲ *Dim sum*

Kong Hotel, the Lao Ching Hing serves marvellous and sparkling Shanghai food. The menu is extensive and includes a good number of vegetarian options. Try the sizzling shrimps for a taste of heaven.

Milano ④

2/F Sun Hung Kai Centre, 30 Harbour Rd, Wanchai

✆ 2598 1222

Ⓜ MTR (Wanchai)

Open: daily 1200–1500, 1800–2400

Reservations essential

All credit cards accepted

Italian

❸❸❸

Up-market place; a very tasty *italiano* with a quality of food and service to match. This is a favourite among Hong Kong residents, particularly for lunch. Milano shares an entrance (and owner) with Saigon. Faultless.

Nice Fragrance Vegetarian Kitchen ⑤

105–7 Thomson Rd, Wanchai

✆ 2838 3067

Ⓜ MTR (Wanchai Exit A3)

Open: daily 1030–2300

Reservations recommended

All credit cards accepted

Takeaway available

Chinese-Vegetarian

❸

A huge and very detailed menu features

beautifully cooked dishes including hotpot, vegetarian shark's fin soup, and a particularly prized soup that is made freshly by the restaurant chefs every day: double boiled yellow fungus and oak mushroom in whole coconut. A strict vegetarian regime is upheld, and peaceful Buddhist music plays in the background. Heavenly.

Patong Thai Restaurant

12–22 Queen's Rd East, Wanchai

✆ 2861 1006

🚇 MTR (Admiralty Exit F via Pacific Place)

Open: daily 1130–1430, 1730–2300

All credit cards accepted

Reservations essential

Thai

❺

Unpretentious and friendly, this positively excels at all the Thai favourites – the *tom yum* soup, the enormous mixed plate of hors-d'oeuvres, the prawns with lemongrass, seafood rice baked in a coconut, are delicious. It is easy to over-order. Whatever you do, do not resist the mango with sticky coconut rice dessert!

Peking Shui Jiao Wong ❼

118 Jaffe Rd, Wanchai

✆ 2527 0289

🚇 MTR (Wanchai Exit A1)

Open: Mon–Sat 0700–2230, Sun 1100–2230

Reservations unnecessary

No credit cards accepted

Takeaway available

Peking

❺

Dumplings galore! *Jiaozi* (fried or boiled dumplings) are the speciality here, filled with different meats and vegetables; the menu is in Chinese so just point to the ones you fancy. Peking dumplings are reputed to be the inspiration for Cantonese *wonton*. A great place to sample basic Beijing cuisine.

Saigon

2/F Sun Hung Kai Centre, 30 Harbour Rd, Wanchai

✆ 2598 7222

🚇 MTR (Wanchai)

Open: daily 1200–1500, 1800–2400

Reservations essential

All credit cards accepted

Vietnamese

❻❻

Delightful and innovative modern Vietnamese dishes, served in a mellow, bamboo interior by attentive and helpful staff. The crispy softshell crab is highly recommended, and there is a large and imaginative vegetarian menu. Enjoy a refreshing baby coconut milk drink while you choose.

The Temple (New Maharani) ❽

G/F 64 Lockhart Rd, Wanchai

✆ 2865 7513

🚇 MTR (Wanchai)

Open: daily 1200–1500, 1800–2330

Reservations recommended for Fri–Sat

All credit cards accepted

Indian

❺

A faithful local clientele raves about this friendly, no frills curry house. Chefs from Nepal and India prepare basic classics to your specification (say how hot you want them). The setting is simple, relaxing and all you need for a great meal with friends. The set lunch, it has to be said, is incredible value.

Viceroy

2/F Sun Hung Kai Centre, 30 Harbour Rd

✆ 2827 7777

🚇 MTR (Wanchai)

Open: 1200–1500, 1800–2300

Reservations essential

All credit cards accepted

Fusion

❻❻

A trendy and popular haunt for Hong Kong locals, with good value, high-quality food where Thai meets Indian. The venue doubles up to provide dancing later on, with dedicated salsa evenings and comedy nights (call to see what's on). Good with groups.

HONG KONG ISLAND: WANCHAI
Bars, cafés and pubs

Café Roma

8–12 Hennessy Rd, Wanchai

MTR (Wanchai)

Open: Mon–Sat 0700–2400

All credit cards accepted

A scrumptious and very good value (English) breakfast is available here; the omelettes are delicious. Later on, a simple but well-thought-out menu offers creative salads with an Italian twist. This modern, stainless steel café turns into a trendy local bar in the evenings.

Chinatown ⑩

G/F Hang Shun Mansions, 78–82 Jaffe Rd, Wanchai

▲ Joe Bananas

MTR (Wanchai)

Open: Mon–Thu 1100–0300, Fri–Sat 1100–0400, Sun 1700–0300

All credit cards accepted

An unashamed and stylish Western slant on old China, where the staff wear smart *cheongsams*, and portraits of Mao Tse Tung gaze across the bar between Chinese lanterns. Food – which is varied and excellent – is served until 2400. Drinking goes on well into the night – an art perfected by the owners, who also run the **Jump and Mad Dogs** in Central.

Coyote ⑪

114–20 Lockhart Rd, Wanchai

MTR (Wanchai Exit C)

Open: daily 1000–0200

All credit cards accepted

The main attraction at this, Hong Kong's first dedicated margarita bar, is the list of over 50 different tequilas. There is a good range of (fairly standard) Mexican dishes, available at the sunshine-yellow bar, or upstairs in the quieter restaurant area.

Healthy Mess ⑫

G/F 51–3 Hennessy Rd, Wanchai

MTR (Wanchai Exit A2)

Open: daily 1030–2300

All credit cards accepted

An enticing assortment of vegetarian sweet and savoury cakes and snacks are proudly displayed in the café window. 'Guaranteed' to be health giving, the message must be: relax; enjoy! Choose between the cafeteria-style room or the adjacent, slightly more formal restaurant. Come here for your special cakes for festivals.

JJ's ⑬

The Grand Hyatt Hotel, 1 Harbour Rd, Wanchai

Open: Mon–Thu 1430–0200
(until 0300 Fri), Sat 1800–
0400

All credit cards accepted

This snazzy, stylish and very up-market bar is one of the 'in' places for Hong Kong's beautiful people. Spread over two floors, live music plays nightly and the bar food is a cut above the rest. Cover charges apply. Happy hour is from 1730 until 2030 Monday to Friday. Dress is smart-casual – no trainers.

Joe Bananas

23 Luard Rd, Wanchai

🕒 MTR (Wanchai)

Open: Mon–Fri 1230–0500,
Sat 1100–0600, Sun 1500–
0500

All credit cards accepted

The place for late-night drinking and dancing; an unpretentious, popular venue (especially with twenty-some-things). The extensive cocktail list, a good range of basic bar food and a disc jockey keep the party going.

The Open Kitchen ⑮

6/F The Hong Kong Arts Centre, 2 Harbour Rd, Wanchai

🕒 Buses to Hong Kong Convention Centre, MTR (Admiralty)

Open: daily 0830–2200

[VISA] 💳 American Express

The fact that the pace here seems, somehow, a little slower, makes this a handy and restoring

▲ Afternoon tea at Tiffin Lounge

stop, whether for a light meal (and an excellent cup of coffee) or a drink at the bar. A few balcony tables offer fabulous harbour views.

Phuket Thai Seafood Restaurant and Bar ⑯

44 Hennessy Rd, Wanchai

🕒 MTR (Wanchai)

Open: daily 1100–2300

[VISA] 💳 ①

Scrumptious and inexpensive Thai food that is served simply, promptly and courteously, in a completely unpretentious little restaurant which deservedly does brisk business.

Sun Chiu Kee ⑰

180 Hennessy Rd, Wanchai

🕒 MTR (Wanchai)

Open: daily 0700–2400

No credit cards accepted

Delicious, inexpensive and sustaining noodles with *wonton* (thin flour wrappers usually filled

with minced pork and shrimp). The Sun Chiu Kee also specialises in *congee*; the thin rice gruel is cooked over several hours and served with ingredients of your choosing – many of which are a little unusual to Western tastes (fish brisket, pig organ or *conpoy*, to name but a few).

Tiffin Lounge ⑱

Mezzanine, The Grand Hyatt Hotel, 1 Harbour Rd, Wanchai

✆ 2588 1234

🕒 MTR (Wanchai)

Open: Mon–Fri 1200–1430,
Mon–Sat 1515–1800, Sun
1545–1800

All credit cards accepted

For sheer indulgence, the Tiffin lunch or the afternoon set tea and cake buffet offer a positively luxurious range of sweet and savoury treats for a (relatively!) modest investment. The 1930s-style interior is a haven. Treat yourself!

HONG KONG ISLAND: WANCHAI

Shops, markets and picnic sites

Shops

Castello del Vino ⑲

10 Anton St, Wanchai

Ⓜ MTR (Wanchai Exit B2)

Open: Mon–Fri 1030–1900,
Sat 1030–1830

All credit cards accepted

A very good choice of
mainly Italian wines
(and also pannini and
sweet Italian cakes),
which are otherwise dif-
ficult to find in the
main supermarkets.

Chinese Arts and Crafts ⑳

China Resources Building, 26
Harbour Rd, Wanchai

Ⓜ MTR (Wanchai)

Open: Mon–Sat 1000–1900,
Sun 1100–1900

All credit cards accepted

One of the largest
branches of CAC. Just
the place to buy
embroidered Chinese
tablemats and table-
cloths, ornate chopsticks
and an infinite variety
of porcelain chopstick
rests and decorative
clay and china teapots.

Herbal and Delicacy Shop ㉑

68 Johnston Rd, Wanchai

Ⓜ MTR (Wanchai Exit A3)

Open: daily 1000–2000

No credit cards accepted

Particularly good qual-
ity dried seafood, such
as scallops, abalone, sea
cucumber, octopus,
Black Sea moss and
other finds, as well as
delicacies with
undoubted but unfath-
omable health-giving
properties.

Juice bar ㉒

61 Luard Rd, Wanchai

Ⓜ MTR (Wanchai Exit B2)

Open: daily 0900–1900

No credit cards accepted

When in need of a quick
energy lift, stop here for
a refreshing, sweet
sugar-cane juice drink,
served from exquisite,
polished brass urns.

Ki Chan Tea Company ㉓

174 Johnston Rd, Wanchai

✆ 2573 0690

Open: daily 1030–1800

No credit cards accepted

If you're near by, this
authentic teashop,
established in 1942, is
just the place to buy
Chinese teas. However,
only a few are labelled
in English, so you may
have to take pot luck!

Kitchen shop ㉔

34 O'Brien Rd, Wanchai

Ⓜ MTR (Wanchai Exit A3)

Open: Mon–Sat 0900–1900

No credit cards accepted

If you've always won-
dered about the secret of
perfect rice – it's a rice
cooker! This place has a
very good range, as well
as tabletop cookers,
should you wish to cre-
ate your own Mongolian
hotpot and Japanese
sukiyaki meals.

▲ Fresh mango stall

Ying Kee Tea Company ㉕

G/F 170 Johnston Rd, Wanchai

🚇 MTR (Wanchai)

Open: Mon–Sat 1000–1900

No credit cards accepted

Another of Hong Kong's more authentic tea-houses, specialising in black teas.

Markets

Tai Yuen Street Market ㉖

Tai Yuen St and Cross St, Wanchai

🚇 MTR (Wanchai)

Open: daily 1000–2000

No credit cards accepted

These streets, just off the main road, are chock-a-block with fresh vegetables and fruit, 1000-year-old eggs, dried meats, poultry and exotic flowers. Early mornings and early evenings are the best times to just follow your nose, and absorb the many sights and smells, as food is prepared in stalls amid a seething throng of busy shoppers.

Kosher food

The Jewish Community Centre runs a home delivery service. All foods are prepared under the supervision of a *mashgiach* and adhere to the strictest level of *kashrut*.
✆ 2598 1718.

Dim sum

Morsels of the heart

If Hong Kong has a signature dish, then it must be *dim sum*. Meaning literally 'touch of the heart' or 'morsels of the heart', *dim sum* are delicate parcels of food served in small portions: ravioli-like dumplings, fluffy buns and pastries steamed, braised or fried and with hundreds of different fillings.

Dim sum is part of the *yum cha* experience. *Yum cha* literally means 'drink tea' but actually implies eating small amounts of food while tea is served and has become a ritual. In fact, it is such an institution in Hong Kong that local people *yum cha* for breakfast, lunch, sometimes dinner and even business deals; families and friends gather, especially at weekends, for what has become a great social gathering. Long queues form in all the best *dim sum* restaurants, which are characterised by noise, bustle and a completely frenetic atmosphere. In all, *dim sum* is not only a major family event, it is also delicious, usually extremely good value and fun.

▲ Super Star

Some of the best *dim sum* restaurants are the noisiest – where it is most difficult to get served! The **Super Star Seafood Restaurants** (*branches at 1/F Tsimshatsui Mansion, 83–97 Nathan Rd, Tsim Sha Tsui; ✆ 2366 0878; ⓐ MTR (Tsim Sha Tsui) and at 4/F Harbour City, 21 Canton Rd, Tsim Sha Tsui; ✆ 2116 2618; ⓐ MTR (Tsim Sha Tsui) and Star Ferry; both open: daily 1030–2400; reservations recommended; all credit cards accepted; ❺*) continue to uphold the finest, most chaotic of *dim sum* atmospheres and are a real treat at weekends. The savoury and sweet snacks are served in steaming bamboo containers piled on trolleys; the idea is to select your dishes by hailing the waiter or waitress and pointing out what you want. Part of the protocol is to lift the lids of the steam baskets to contemplate the food critically; if you don't like the look of it, just say no! This behaviour will be considered perfectly normal; it is part of the proper etiquette. However, this is easier said than done in the noisy and somehow shambolic environment of a Chinese restaurant at rush hour; it always seems that it's the wrong trolley that comes round, so you may find it easier to tick at least a few of your choices on the menu at the outset.

As always with Chinese food, the dishes are meant to be

shared. Each bamboo basket contains three or four *dim sum*, allowing you to sample as many as possible. But don't be fooled and don't order all at once: *dim sum* are small but filling, so it is wise to begin with just a few dishes and order more as you eat. There are no particular rules (other than reserving sweet dishes to last). The classic favourites are *har gau* – plump, translucent dumplings filled with shrimp; *siu mai* – minced pork and shrimp wrapped in thin flour wrappers; *char siu bau* – delicious steamed fluffy buns filled with barbecued pork (which are a very popular choice for breakfast); *woo gok* – deep fried *taro* dumplings; and steamed glutinous rice wrapped in lotus leaves.

▲ Dim sum

One of the most delightful speciality restaurants is **Dim Sum** (*63 Sing Woo Rd, Happy Valley; ✆ 2834 8893; ◉ MTR Causeway Bay; open: daily 1100–1630, 1800–2230; reservations not possible Sat–Sun lunch; all credit cards accepted;* ❸❸). The stunning interior is classic 1930s rosewood with marble-top tables and charming private booths for small groups.

> **... ravioli-like dumplings, fluffy buns and pastries steamed, braised or fried and with hundreds of different fillings ...**

Reservations are recommended and long queues form at weekends. In spite of its popularity and style, Dim Sum offers incredible value and an experience from a bygone era. The **Luk Yu Tea House** (*see page 11*) is another historic *dim sum* establishment serving staunchly traditional dishes.

You could be forgiven for thinking that *dim sum* are quick and easy snack foods – but in fact, they require skill and patience to make. There are hundreds of different types, and they must all be made freshly and by hand; in fact their preparation is so time consuming that a restaurant must normally restrict its menu to twenty or thirty varieties. Nowadays, Hong Kong *dim sum* chefs build their reputation on creating new tastes, using subtly different and luxurious ingredients. Wherever you dine, whether at a street stall where the *siu mai* may be threaded on a skewer, or at the **Lai Ching Heen Restaurant** (*see page 59*), one of Hong Kong's finest Cantonese restaurants, *dim sum* is quintessentially Hong Kong and one mustn't leave without the experience!

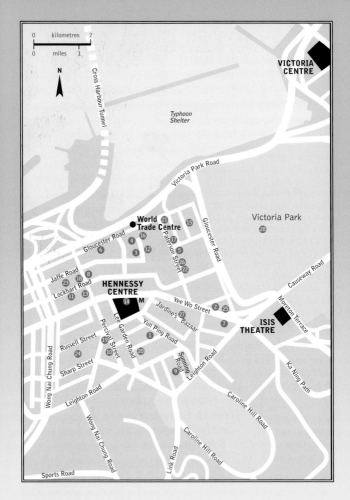

Hong Kong Island: Causeway Bay and Happy Valley

Somehow the mix of old and new makes Causeway Bay seem busier and noisier than the rest of Hong Kong. Full of restaurants and department stores (sometimes known as 'mini Tokyo'), it is great for multi-cultural, pan-Asian cuisine.

HONG KONG ISLAND: CAUSEWAY BAY AND HAPPY VALLEY
Restaurants

IChiBan

G/F 21 Lan Fong Rd,
Causeway Bay

✆ 2890 7580

🅜 MTR (Causeway Bay
Exit A)

Open: daily 1800–0200

Reservations recommended

All credit cards accepted

Japanese

⑧ ⑤

A wonderfully authentic, down-to-earth Japanese with very unfussy décor: the main business here is good food. Try the *yakitori* or *sashimi* (succulent slices of uncooked fish) washed down with *sake* served at the perfect temperature. Ask for a little private booth when you book. Restrained elegance.

Kung Tak Lam

G/F–1/F 31 Yee Wo St,
Causeway Bay

✆ 2890 3127

🅜 MTR (Causeway Bay
Exit E)

Open: daily 1100–2300

Reservations recommended

All credit cards accepted

Takeaway available; beer and
soft drinks only

Shanghai-Vegetarian

A plentiful and healthy vegetarian menu which steadfastly avoids monosodium glutamate. The deep-fried *taro* is a must, and the roast goose their most famous dish (typically, many dishes are presented as 'mock meat'). Non-vegetarians love this place too!

Myung Ga Korean Restaurant ❸

Podium 3 World Trade
Centre, 280 Gloucester Rd,
Causeway Bay

▲ Silky fowl

✆ 2882 5056

 MTR (Causeway Bay Exit D)

Open: daily 1200–1500, 1800–2300

Reservations recommended

All credit cards accepted

Korean

❸❺

An eye-boggling display of plastic food at the entrance – which turns out to be quite useful in deciding whether to go for Korean barbecue or hotpot, which are the specialities here. The tabletop seafood barbecue is a feast in every way and can cater for any number. Crisp, clean, friendly and justifiably popular.

Oscar's Australian ❹

Podium 3 World Trade Centre, 280 Gloucester Rd, Causeway Bay

✆ 2861 1511

🅜 MTR (Causeway Bay Exit D)

Open: daily 1200–0030

Reservations recommended

All credit cards accepted

Australian

❸❺

Bright, breezy and welcoming, this is grown-up Aussie, offering such delights as melt-in-the-mouth barramundi fillets with lemon and dill, and inventive Australian *dim sum* – don't ask, just try it

(*Sun only, 1230–1530*). Sophisticated and beautifully presented. Ask for a window overlooking the Hong Kong Yacht Club.

Paper Moon ❺

Shop B, G/F 8 Kingston St, Causeway Bay

✆ 2881 5070

🅜 MTR (Causeway Bay Exit E)

Open: Mon–Thu 1130–0100, Fri–Sat 1130–0200, Sun 1130–2400

Reservations unnecessary

All credit cards accepted

American

❸❺

Great for kids: one can't pretend that Paper

Moon is in any way (cooking or décor) subtle! The emphasis is on making food fun, and it succeeds. There is an excellent children's menu. Beware the enormous portions!

Rangoon Restaurant

265 Gloucester Rd, Causeway Bay

☎ 2893 2281

🚇 MTR (Causeway Bay Exit D1)

Open: daily 1130–2330

Reservations recommended

💳 💳 American Express

Takeaway available

Burmese

💲

The Burmese food – a wonderfully delicate blend, with subtle Thai and Indian influences – is excellent here (although the setting is perhaps on the dull side), and the range of vegetarian food is quite extensive. Don't be put off by the unconvincing photo-menu.

Regal Chiu Chow ⑦

2/F Regal International Hotel, 68 Yee Wo St, Causeway Bay

☎ 2837 1786

🚇 MTR (Causeway Bay Exit F)

Open: Mon–Sat 1100–1500, 1800–2300, from 1000 Sun

Reservations essential

All credit cards accepted

Chiu Chow

💲💲

Best to go in as large a group as possible, to sample lots of the excellent Chiu Chow dishes … and make a truly convincing mess of the crisply ironed table cloths. The menu of special delicacies includes reasonably priced bird's nest dishes and traditional Chiu Chow marinated goose. The real McCoy.

She Wong Yee ⑧

24 Percival St, Causeway Bay

☎ 2893 1107

🚇 MTR (Causeway Bay Exit C)

Open: daily 1130–2400

Reservations unnecessary

No credit cards accepted

Chinese

💲

One of Hong Kong's oldest snake restaurants; the counter is adorned with pickled lizards, bottles of snake wine and even live snakes in a case. Snake is a gastronomic adventure; it really is delicious, and this is the place to try it. The snake soup is recommended for beginners, and guaranteed to convert you. Be brave!

Snow Garden ⑨

2/F Ming An Plaza, 8 Sunning Rd, Causeway Bay

☎ 2881 6837

🚇 MTR (Causeway Bay Exit F)

Open: daily 1130–1500, 1800–2300

Reservations recommended

All credit cards accepted

Shanghai

💲💲

The Snow Garden serves Shanghai *dim sum* all day, and pork dumplings baked in bamboo (*siu long pao*) are a favourite. Set lunches are good value, though one can spend a little more, with wine, in the evenings. The most popular dishes are

Robatayaki I CHI BAN

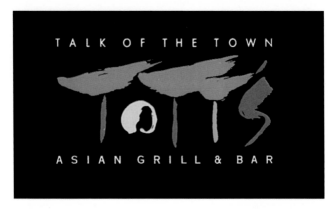

stir-fried freshwater shrimps and drunken pigeon, marinated for hours in rice wine.

Sorabol ⑩

17/F Lee Theatre Plaza, 99 Percival St, Causeway Bay

✆ 2881 6823

🔘 MTR (Causeway Bay Exit A)

Open: daily 1200–1430, 1800–2230

Reservations recommended

All credit cards accepted

Korean

❸❸

Very popular with Koreans, the *gooi* barbecue and *shabu shabu* hotpot are excellent here. Gaze out from the 17th floor over the sharply contrasting new and old, high- and low-rises of Causeway Bay. Smart, but very unpretentious and consistently good.

Sze Chuan Lau ⑪

G/F 466 Lockhart Rd

✆ 2891 9027

🔘 MTR (Causeway Bay Exit B)

Open: daily 1130–2330

Reservations essential

💳 💳 American Express

Szechuan

❸❸❸

With lovely wooden-panelled rooms, this is a favourite of many locals. The staff in this old Hong Kong institution always recommend their smoked duck or pigeon with camphor and tea. Szechuan food can be spicy, but hot dishes are clearly indicated on the menu. Busy (to put it mildly) and relatively pricey, it is none the less possible to eat here quite reasonably. A good assortment of Chinese wines is available.

Tott's Asian Grill and Bar ⑫

34/F The Excelsior Hotel, 281 Gloucester Rd, Causeway Bay

✆ 2837 6786

🔘 MTR (Causeway Bay Exit D)

Open: daily 1200–1430; Sun–Thu 1700–0100, Fri–Sat 1700–0200

Reservations recommended

All credit cards accepted

International-Fusion

❸❸❸

Tott's (Talk Of The Town) blends heavenly Eastern and Western cuisines in perfect harmony (just try the naan breads with smoked salmon to tickle your tastebuds). The experience is topped with stunning panoramic views across the harbour. Live music and dancing begins at around 2130 (*Mon–Sat*) for the glitzy and the glamorous. Well fused!

Café Eos 13

Shop B, G/F 23–5 Percival St, Causeway Bay

🅜 MTR (Causeway Bay Exit B)

Open: daily 1100–2400

Artfully presented as a little English teashop, with English teas and sandwiches, light snacks and newspapers to read as you rest from the frantic energy of Causeway Bay.

Chitose 14

Basement 3, Mitsukoshi, Hennessy Centre, 500 Hennessy Rd, Causeway Bay

🅜 MTR (Causeway Bay Exit F)

Open: daily 1000–2300

All credit cards accepted

In the (relative) calm of one of the smaller Japanese department stores, the Chitose café offers light snacks with an international flavour and coffees.

Delicious Kitchen 15

Shop 8, 9–11 Cleveland St, Causeway Bay

🅜 MTR (Causeway Bay Exit E)

Open: daily 1000–2330

American Express

Not the place to have a leisurely meal, the turnover of business is fast, and you may have to queue to get in – but it's worth it. The Shanghai noodles, rice

▲ Dicken's Bar

dishes (pork ribs with vegetables) and sweet pancakes are lethal!

Dicken's Bar 16

The Excelsior Hotel, 281 Gloucester Rd, Causeway Bay

🔘 MTR (Causeway Bay Exit D)

Open: daily 1200–2330

All credit cards accepted

A popular port-of-call for office workers in the evening, and a comfy pub with good British grub (such as steak and kidney pie, bangers and mash, burgers and salads), but which doubles very effectively as a sports bar (with a large screen television and walls lined with local sports team pictures).

Island Seafood and Oyster Bar 17

Shop C, Towning Mansion, 50–6 Paterson St, Causeway Bay

🔘 MTR (Causeway Bay Exit E)

Open: daily 1200–2400

All credit cards accepted

This oyster bar is something of an oasis, as it somehow manages to create a relaxed, easy-going atmosphere. Not only for oyster-lovers, but there is a good range of seafood dishes too.

The Jump 18

7/F Causeway Bay Plaza, 463 Lockhart Rd, Causeway Bay

🔘 MTR (Causeway Bay Exit C)

Open: Mon–Tue and Thu 1200–0200, Sun, Wed and Fri 1200–0300

💳 💳 American Express

Lots of gimmicks at this American bar-restaurant, popular with a funky, hip, young crowd. Burgers, salads and pastas served in a ship's-cabin interior; dancing starts at 2230.

Kung Wo Tung 19

87 Percival St, Causeway Bay

🔘 MTR (Causeway Bay Exit A)

Open: daily 1000–1900

No credit cards accepted

A handy stop for a reviving sugar cane juice drink or, for the intrepid and the adventurous, a cup of hot jelly made from, among other things, turtle shell and aromatic herbs. Served from a massive, heated cauldron and eaten with lots of sugar, this slightly bitter potion has health-giving and aphrodisiac qualities.

Muse Café 20

10 Lan Fong Rd, Causeway Bay

🔘 MTR (Causeway Bay Exit A)

Open: daily 1000–2100

No credit cards accepted

Handy for a coffee or a freshly made sandwich if you're near by. The café is tiny with only a few stools, but is a quiet and friendly place to rest your shop-weary feet.

Stix 21

310 Gloucester Rd, Causeway Bay

☎ 2839 3397

🔘 MTR (Causeway Bay Exit E)

Open: Mon–Wed 1700–0100, Thu–Sat 1700–0200 or later

All credit cards accepted

Popular with a youngish crowd, and always heaving after work, this is a lively bar normally with loud music. The food (substantial American grills and sandwiches) is good and, strangely, often overlooked.

Young's Café 22

Shop 6–7, JP Plaza, 22–36 Paterson St, Causeway Bay

🔘 MTR (Causeway Bay)

Open: daily 1200–2400

💳 💳

If Haagen Dazs hasn't taken your custom already, this is an indulgent place to take a break, with ice creams and milkshakes in fateful abundance.

HONG KONG ISLAND: CAUSEWAY BAY AND HAPPY VALLEY
Shops, markets and picnic sites

Shops

The Best Tea Company Ltd ㉓

G02 Causeway Bay Plaza, 463 Lockhart Rd, Causeway Bay

🔵 MTR (Causeway Bay Exit C)

Open: daily 1200–2200

All credit cards accepted

A specialist teashop with a range of inexpensive earthenware teapots. Sit quietly and sample some of the teas before you buy.

City Super ㉔

Basement One, Times Sq., Causeway Bay

🔵 MTR (Causeway Bay Exit A)

Open: Sun–Thu 1030–2200, Fri–Sat 1030–2300

[???]

Supermarket-cum-delicatessen with gloriously presented fresh food, and all the essentials and luxuries you could possibly want.

CRC Department Store Ltd ㉕

Lok Sing Centre, 31 Yee Wo St, Causeway Bay

🔵 MTR (Causeway Bay Exit F)

Open: daily 1000–1830

No credit cards accepted

A rich source of authentic mainland Chinese products, from teas, rice and grape wines, rice-based liqueurs, herbs and medicines, as well as clothing, bedding, luggage …

Mitsukoshi bakery ⑭

Basement 3, Mitsukoshi, Hennessy Centre, 500 Hennessy Rd, Causeway Bay

🔵 MTR (Causeway Bay Exit F)

Open: daily 1000–2300

All credit cards accepted

Here, as at most Japanese department stores, you'll find an array of self-service sweet and savoury buns and freshly baked bread. You haven't lived till you've tried a Japanese croissant!

Yue Hwa Chinese Products Emporium ㉖

24 Paterson St, Causeway Bay

🔵 MTR (Causeway Bay Exit E)

Open: daily 1000–2200

No credit cards accepted

One of the five branches of this mainland Chinese emporium. Dried foods, teas, alcoholic drinks and goodies to take home.

Markets

Jardines Bazaar Market ㉗

Jardines Bazaar, Causeway Bay

🔵 MTR (Causeway Bay Exit F)

Open: daily 1100–1930

No credit cards accepted

One of the oldest street markets on Hong Kong Island, the streets just off Yee Wo Street become filled with an assortment of tropical fruits and Chinese vegetables and meat, as well as basic clothing.

Picnic sites

Victoria Park ㉘

Causeway Bay

🔵 MTR (Causeway Bay)

Home to a popular flower market, and serenely alive in the early morning with *tai chi* disciples. Victoria Park is occasionally taken over for major sporting events, and is a magnet at festival times – particularly the Mid-Autumn Festival. At any time, though, it is a welcome haven amid the din and bustle of Causeway Bay.

All the tea in China

Upholding tradition

As soon as you sit down in a Chinese restaurant you are offered tea. China's national drink, tea is not merely a thirst quencher, but a traditional welcome, and the very essence of Chinese culture.

Its virtues have been enjoyed for thousands of years, and its central role in China's trade history is told eloquently at the **Museum of Tea Ware** (*Flagstaff House, 10 Cotton Tree Dr., Central; ✆ 2869 0690; ⊕ MTR (Admiralty); open: Thu–Tue 1000–1700; admission free*). The museum itself is housed in the former residence of Hong Kong's Commander-in-Chief in the 1840s, and has a gift shop. Its collection of teapots and tea-making utensils dates back to the 5th century BC and really brings out the importance of tea in Chinese trade. Together with silk and porcelain, trade in tea had major implications for the country's economy. Its popularity was unprecedented: first drunk at the Imperial Court, it rapidly spread to all classes of society and to neighbouring countries such as Japan and Russia. Tea first reached Europe in the 17th century, and by the 18th had become an established institution in England.

China's three main teas (black, oolong and green tea) all come from the same plant but are processed differently. **Black tea** is oxidised (the fermentation process) before being dried by firing (rather like stir-frying); **oolong** is oxidised half way; and **green tea** is dried immediately without being oxidised at all. The results couldn't be more different. **Keemun** and **Pu'er**, the best known of Chinese black teas, are mellow and smooth, and just get better and better through ageing and maturation. Oolong is yellowish brown in colour and has a very intense flavour and a fragrant lingering aftertaste. **Phoenix Shui Sin** is one of the most popular oolong teas in Guangzhou. Green tea is invariably light and fragrant and is probably the most popular tea in China; **Dragon Well** (lung ching) is a favourite. One of the easiest ways to find your own favourites is to opt for the little assortment boxes from **Yue Hwa Chinese Products Emporium** (*see page 45*).

Given its early history in medicine, there is, not surprisingly, **a tea for every ailment**; it helps the digestion, stimulates the brain and is fundamentally sustaining.

▲ Teapots for sale

Pu'er is renowned for preventing cholesterol accumulation, oolong for lowering fat in the blood; green tea is still the subject of several medical studies for its alleged properties in combating the development of cancer. **Ginseng** is added as a fortifying and aphrodisiac potion. It is also used in cooking: duck cooked in camphor and green tea is a famous Shanghainese speciality and eggs boiled in tea are available from most markets.

Hong Kong **traditional teahouses**, *chah geui* (literally 'little tea huts'), used to crowd Western District (Sheung Wan). This is where people would drink tea (*yum cha*) and eat *dim sum* while reading their papers. Only a few establishments, such as the **Luk Yu Tea House** (*see page 11*), named after the Tang Dynasty scholar who wrote China's most comprehensive work on tea, still uphold the true tradition. Instead, British afternoon tea has taken over, and in most of Hong Kong's grand hotels cream teas, finger sandwiches and even full-blown tiffin are now standard features. Perhaps more curious is how Western influence has resulted in the popularity of 'milk tea', a brew of tea and the condensed milk that is a mainstay of so many Chinese desserts. Milk tea is *the* standard brew *at dai pai dong* street cafés, and *cha chan teng*, literally, 'salons for tea and Western food'.

Like wine, the pleasure is in getting to know the different

▲ Tea stall

appellations, colours and flavours of tea. Specialists such as **The Best Tea Company Ltd** (*see page 45*) will receive you as a guest, invite you to sit and sample different varieties, initiate you into the secrets of a perfect brew, and allow you to linger over the aromas and flavours of each one. You will want to know when the leaves were harvested, whether – as the best teas are – they have been hand-rolled, whether they have been scented with fruits, or perhaps flowers … Compared to the Japanese tea ceremony, tea preparation in Hong Kong is remarkably practical and workmanlike. The best teapots are made of low-fired clay, which hold a perfect temperature, and are invariably small to avoid over-stewing.

Aromatic, mellow or fragrant tea certainly arouses the same passions as wine. Learning its subtleties takes years of comparison, tasting, experiment and pleasure – so get brewing!

> Oolong is yellowish brown in colour and has a very intense flavour and a fragrant lingering aftertaste.

Hong Kong Island: Southside

Much of Southside is what you might expect Hong Kong to have resembled 80 years ago. Apart from the major fishing community of Aberdeen (Heung Kong Tsai, literally 'Little Hong Kong'), which is now increasingly built up and industrial, most of the bays are (relatively) unpopulated, with eateries full of character, catering largely to local residents and weekend visitors.

HONG KONG ISLAND: SOUTHSIDE
Restaurants

Beaches (Stanley's Italian) ❶

92B Stanley Main Rd, Stanley

✆ 2813 7313

🚍 Buses 6, 6A and 260 from Central

Open: daily 1100–2300

Reservations unnecessary

All credit cards accepted

Italian

❺

The idea here is to create your own dish by first choosing the pasta, followed by the sauce, and then as many ingredients as you want. Laid back and good value; ideal after a hard day on the beach.

Black Sheep ❷

452 Shek O Village, Shek O

✆ 2809 2021

🚍 Bus 9

Open: Tue–Fri 1930–2400, Sat–Sun 1300–2400

Reservations unnecessary

No credit cards accepted

International

❺❺

Some innovative and delicious food, in a no-frills-whatsoever atmosphere. This is a popular place with locals; the salads are wonderfully refreshing and the simple, grilled, fresh fish a must.

Jumbo Palace Floating Restaurant ❸

Shum Wan, Wong Chuk Hang, Aberdeen harbour

✆ 2553 9111

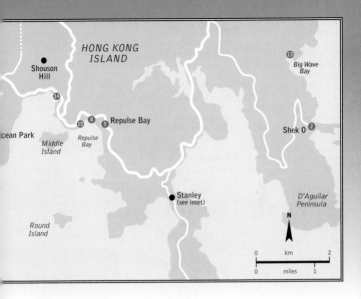

HONG KONG ISLAND

Shouson Hill

Repulse Bay

Ocean Park

Middle Island

Repulse Bay

Big Wave Bay

Shek O

Stanley
(see inset)

D'Aguilar Peninsula

Round Island

N

| 0 | km | 2 |
| 0 | miles | 1 |

 Buses 7, 70 and 70M from Central or Admiralty, and free boat – or own hired *kai do* (sampan) – from Shum Wan Pier Road

Open: daily 1100–2300; *dim sum* 1100–1700

Reservations unnecessary for lunch, Reservations recommended for dinner

All credit cards accepted

Cantonese-Seafood

Treat yourself to a fun experience amid outlandish décor, even if dinner is a little overpriced. You'll be invited to pick out the exact fish you'd like to eat, from the 'seafood exhibition'. The *dim sum* lunch, however, is good value, and all the better

for the thrill of the sampan trip through Aberdeen harbour to get there. Go on, be a tourist!

Middle Kingdom ❹

UG/F Exhibition Hall Bldg, Middle Kingdom, Ocean Park, Shum Wan Rd, Tai Shue Wan, Aberdeen

☎ 2814 9272

Buses 43X and 70

Open: daily 1200–2000

Reservations unnecessary

All credit cards accepted

Cantonese

An ideal break from a visit to the Disney-like Ocean Park – a day's worth of family entertainment

amusement park to ocean theatre (performing dolphins), aquarium and 'living theatre' performances of Chinese culture. The Middle Kingdom offers all the favourites, and not surprisingly is often filled with families. The grilled crispy eel is particularly recommended.

Shek O Chinese Thai Seafood ❷

303 Shek O Village, Shek O

☎ 2809 4426

Bus 9

Open: daily 1100–2200

Reservations recommended

No credit cards accepted

Thai-Chinese-Seafood

This friendly restaurant, located just by the main bus stop, serves up generous helpings of fairly standard but tasty curries, seafood, vegetable and rice dishes. Note: it gets very busy at weekends, with those exploring the popular Dragon's Back countryside walk, and even members of the nearby Golf Club on their way home.

Spices ❺

The Arcade, The Repulse Bay, 109 Repulse Bay Rd
☎ 2812 2711
🚌 Buses 6, 6A and 260 from Central
Open: daily 1030–2230
Reservations recommended
All credit cards accepted
Fusion
❷❺

Spices from all over Asia are brought together in a range of innovative dishes, based on classics from Indonesia, Thailand, Malaysia, Japan, India… and Arabia. Good for a *soupçon* of adventure and a fabulous sea view; try the Thai fried chicken in *pandanas* leaves.

Stanley Restaurant ❻

Upper G/F, 52–6 Stanley Main Rd
☎ 2813 7998
🚌 Buses 6, 6A and 260 from Central
Open: daily 0700–2230
Reservations not allowed
No credit cards accepted

Cantonese-Thai
❺

Bustling diner catering to the Stanley Market traders as well as shoppers, and still alive with the din of happy eating in mid-afternoon. Simple noodle- and rice-based dishes, soups or more adventurous concoctions, with an extensive menu translated into English. A takeaway hotline is advertised.

Stanley's French ❶

1/F and 2/F Oriental Bldg, 90B Stanley Main Rd, Stanley
☎ 2813 8873
🚌 Buses 6, 6A and 260 from Central
Open: daily 0900–2400
Reservations essential
All credit cards accepted
French
❶❶❶

A table on the veranda gives diners a delightful view over Stanley Bay, just the place to watch the sun set. The traditional French cuisine is tinged with a little Oriental influence, for example in the delicious soya flavoured black cod on braised leeks. The wine list is top notch. Romantic.

Stanley's Oriental ❶

G/F and 4/F Oriental Bldg, 90B Stanley Main Rd, Stanley
☎ 2813 9988
🚌 Buses 6, 6A and 260 from Central
Open: daily 0900–2400
Reservations recommended
All credit cards accepted
Fusion
❶❶

There is a relaxed snack bar on the ground floor. The restaurant on the 4th floor offers an eclectic oriental menu and spectacular views over the bay. Marvellous roast duck in coconut green curry sauce and all the traditional Thai dishes, Indian curries and tandoori (specify how hot you'd like it), Creole and Cajun touches. You must try

▲ Jumbo Palace Floating Restau

the coconut *crème brûlee* for dessert.

Tables 88 7

88 Stanley Village Rd, Stanley

☏ 2813 6262

🚌 Buses 6, 6A and 260 from Central

Open: daily 1130–2300

Reservations essential

All credit cards accepted

International

❸❸❸

Set in the old Police Station, this Designed (with a capital 'D') restaurant is a trendy, dungeonesque

enchanted forest of a place. Well worth the trip out of town; go for dinner rather than lunch. A large and imaginative menu: the sear-fried Norwegian salmon is a real treat, the grill is always popular and the desserts are simply wicked.

Tai Fat Hau Restaurant 8

Sea View Bldg, The Repulse Bay, 16 Beach Rd

☏ 2812 2113

🚌 Buses 6, 6A and 260 from Central

Open: daily 1100–2330

All credit cards accepted

Reservations unnecessary

Cantonese

❸

The large breezy dining room and terrace could not be more convenient after (or indeed, during) a day on the beach. Fresh seafood, a solid all-round menu and a barbecue in the summer. Just the job.

The Verandah Restaurant 5

The Arcade, The Repulse Bay, 109 Repulse Bay Rd

☏ 2812 2722

▲ Aberdeen harbour

🚌 Buses 6, 6A and 260 from Central

Open: daily lunch 1200–1430, high tea 1500–1730, dinner 1830–2230

Reservations recommended

All credit cards accepted

French

⑤⑤⑤

Quiet and sophisticated, the impeccable service will make you feel well looked after whether it's a special dinner or a discreet business lunch.

The classics are all there and exquisite, though do try the pan-fried escalope of goose liver with mushroom charlotte. A 'special selection' supplements the classy, mainly French wine list. Colonial evocations.

Welcome Garden ❷

770 Shek O Village, Shek O

☎ 2809 2836

🚌 Bus 9

Open: daily 1130–2230

Reservations unnecessary

No credit cards accepted

Szechuan

⑤

A relaxing end to the day with freshly prepared Szechuan staples such as chilli or garlic beef, served in generous helpings. The staff are friendly and this remains a popular stop with visitors and locals alike. Laid back.

珍　寶　海　鮮　舫
JUMBO FLOATING RESTAURANT

HONG KONG ISLAND: SOUTHSIDE
Bars, cafés and pubs

The Bamboo Bar

The Arcade, The Repulse Bay, 109 Repulse Bay Rd

Buses 6, 6A and 260 from Central

Open: daily 1200–2230

All credit cards accepted

It's difficult not to be lured in to this comfortable and relaxing bar, with its cane chairs and aura of times gone by ... the same, re-created, quasi-colonial atmosphere as the rest of The Repulse Bay. Smart.

Délifrance

Stanley Market St, Stanley

Buses 6, 6A and 260 from Central

Open: daily 0800–2100

No credit cards accepted

Larger than many of Hong Kong's Delifrance outlets, the tables here are much welcomed by the shopping-weary. Baguettes, sandwiches, filled croissants and pastries are on offer.

Lord Stanley's Sports Bar

92A Stanley Main Rd, Stanley

Buses 6, 6A and 260 from Central

Open: daily 1100–2300 or later

All credit cards accepted

Aptly named, with continuous (but normally unobtrusive) televised sports events. A reassuring range of draught beers including Caffreys and Carlsberg, and a nice choice of wines by the glass (otherwise normally an expensive option in Hong Kong). Very good pub fare. Chill out here after the thirsty work of bargain hunting.

The Palm Court Café and Cake Shop

G110 The Arcade, The Repulse Bay, 109 Repulse Bay Rd

Buses 6, 6A and 260 from Central

Open: daily 1200–1800

All credit cards accepted

An array of generously filled baguettes and sandwiches to eat in the adjacent open-air terraced courtyard, or to take away for your own beach picnic. The cakes and chocolates are luxurious.

The Village Bar and Restaurant

Upper G/F 40–2 Stanley Main Rd, Stanley

Buses 6, 6A and 260 from Central

Open: daily 1000–2200

Another handy stop or break from a hard day's shopping, this fully licensed little café serves basic, inexpensive sandwiches, burgers and Malay/Indonesian snacks.

HONG KONG ISLAND: SOUTHSIDE
Shops, markets and picnic sites

Shops

7 Eleven 🄻

Stanley Market St, Stanley

🄟 Buses 6, 6A and 260 from Central

Open: daily 0700–2300

Tiny but convenient: soft drinks, cigarettes and a few of life's essentials. Branches, as the name suggests, are open till late, and are dotted all over Hong Kong.

Wellcome supermarket 🄓

The Arcade, The Repulse Bay, 109 Repulse Bay Rd

🄟 Buses 6, 6A and 260 from Central

Open: daily 0830–2000

All credit cards accepted

One in a large chain of general purpose convenience stores, and incidentally, one of the few supermarkets to sell tonic water, which is in curiously short supply in Hong Kong's smaller convenience store chains.

Markets

Stanley Market 🄬

Stanley Market St, Stanley

🄟 Buses 6, 6A and 260 from Central

Open: daily 0800–1900

No credit cards accepted

Stanley Market is really famous for the shops – mostly geared to tourists and *gweilos* (foreign devils) – selling silk blouses, jeans, ski wear, trainers, luggage, Chinese arts and crafts, souvenirs and so on. One of the few fruit and vegetable shops in this area lies at the entrance to the market, and also sells exotic flowers and small shrubs.

Picnic sites

Big Wave Bay 🄭

Big Wave Bay Rd

🄟 Bus 9, a 30-min walk from Shek-O

A sheltered bay with lifeguards on duty and a shark net (common on most of Hong Kong's beaches, to ensure that swimmers are safe), this is a popular destination for a full day on the beach. Little beach awnings can be hired, for those who get there early.

Deep Water Bay 🄮

Deep Water Bay Rd

🄟 Buses 6 and 6A

Very popular, with the ubiquitous barbecue pits and beachside cafeterias and soft-drink shops, Deep Water Bay is otherwise quite secluded. The private golf club provides a serene, old-world backdrop to the throngs of bathers who flock here on summer weekends.

The Repulse Bay 🄯

Repulse Bay Rd

🄟 Buses 6 or 6A

Named after the HMS *Repulse*, people still talk

▲ St Stephen's Beach

about 'The Bay That Used to House The Famous, Colonial, Repulse Bay Hotel'. It was pulled down, however, in 1982; the complex that now stands in its place makes a good attempt at recreating a long-gone era, but shares the bay with a massive set of apartment blocks. The beach is an incredibly popular (for which, read unbelievably densely populated) swimming and barbecuing spot in the summer. A smart temple, with statues of Kwan Yum (Goddess of Mercy) and Tin Hau (Goddess of Fishermen), stands at the east of the Bay. Nearby **Middle Bay**, and **South Bay** (Nam Wan) are smaller and tend to be less crowded.

Shek-O Village

Shek-O

🚌 Bus 9

On a tiny headland, there are delightful beaches on both sides of Shek-O Village, with a popular barbecue spot to the south. The more adventurous weekend picnickers trek out to the end of the **Tai Tau Chau headland** for their picnics, or use Shek-O as the final destination in the **Dragon's Back** hilltop walk through the Shek-O Country Park from high above Chai Wan.

Stanley beaches ❶

Stanley

🚌 Buses 6, 6A and 260 from Central

Stanley Main Beach is a good spot to relax after

serious bargain hunting in the market – or before visiting the temple to Tin Hau, Goddess of Fishermen, at the western end of the village. If you're here during the Dragon Boat Festival in June, Stanley Beach is the place to be. On the other side of the peninsula, **St Stephen's Beach** is even more relaxing. Stanley itself is worth exploring: it was already a thriving village when the British arrived in 1841 and was later established as a military garrison. Today, the beautifully maintained **Military Cemetery**, just to the north of the village, encapsulates much of the history; the fort has been converted into luxury apartments.

Tastes of Asia

Eastern specialities

Spoiled for choice! Hong Kong has attracted some of the finest chefs from across all of Asia; it is a melting pot of culinary ingenuity. Here, like almost nowhere on earth, one can leap whole nations in a single stroll down the street. So, if you are intent on sampling the Asia beyond Hong Kong, where do you begin?

INDIA

... offers a tantalising diversity of food styles, from the rich, Persian-influenced cuisine of the north (with *tandoor* dry-roasted foods and lots of meat, dried fruits and nuts, in sweet, spice-laden creamy sauces) to the thinner, colourful curries of the south, or the fiery hot spices of Portuguese-influenced Goa. Curries are sweetened with spices such as cardamom, clove, cinnamon, nutmeg and mace, and hints of saffron; made hot with curry and chilli; and often enriched with yoghurt or coconut paste. Hindu religion forbids the eating of beef. A typical meal for two would comprise one or two meat curry dishes, a vegetable dish, white rice and naan or some other form of bread. Alcohol is rarely drunk; instead, *lassi* is a popular drink made of coconut and fruit juices.

INDONESIA

... consists of over 13,000 fertile islands – the Spice Islands – with a rich history of Indian, Arabic and later Dutch trade. Its innumerable different cooking styles almost seem to mirror the multitude of islands. Most of Indonesia follows Islam, except for Bali, which is largely Hindu and where you can therefore readily find pork in restaurants – as well as famous *bettutu* duck, wrapped in spices and banana leaves and slowly baked over charcoal. The Arabic influence is responsible for Indonesian skewered meats: *satay*; the Dutch culinary legacy, on the other hand, is *rijstaffel*, or rice table, a feast of 30 or more dishes served to guests at a long table.

JAPAN

... is the epitome of artistic perfection in its preparation, cooking and presentation. Japanese cooks prize their artistic skills as highly as their culinary abilities. Dishes are striking in their elegance, simplicity and representation of nature, and seem to be inspired by Zen-Buddhism: sauces are normally thin; batter is light and airy; seasoning is delicate if salty. One of the important flavours in Japanese cuisine is *kombu*, a mineral-rich giant kelp from the coast off Hokkaido. Drinking *sake* with your meal only adds to the sense of ceremony; this beguiling rice wine should be warmed to 42°C (108°F) and is served in tiny porcelain cups.

KOREA

... has an extreme climate and a warm and sustaining cuisine to match. The abundant use of chillies and pepper produces strong, dominant flavours. Noodles are a mainstay, and many dishes (commonly soup-based and stews) use beef, seafood and beans, supplemented by eggplant, lots of cabbage, *daikon* radish and cucumbers. The pickled cabbage, *kim chee*, is an essential accompaniment to any meal, especially the tabletop barbecue meal, *bulgogi*.

▲ Korean barbecue

MALAYSIA

... has a heart-warming cuisine born of a rich trading history, and combines Malay, Indian and Chinese cultures. Mildly flavoured Chinese dishes (based largely on Cantonese cuisine) may be spiced up with a dash of chilli; or a mild curry may be made more aromatic with sweet Indian spices. Food is normally eaten using the thumb and first two fingers of the right hand, and banana leaves serve as plates. Pork is forbidden, as Malaysia is an Islamic nation.

THAILAND

... is an adventure into the unknown, with all the best of Malay, Indian and Chinese cuisine, pepped up with fiery and colourful spices and vegetables. The seafood dishes tend to herald from the south, and the meat dishes from the landlocked north. Typically, rice will be served at the start with a soup, salad and stir-fried dish, all at once; main meat or seafood dishes will follow and fruit normally closes the meal. Thai food can be very, very hot, and part of the adventure at many Thai restaurants is to add as much heat as you want from a huge tray of different spices.

VIETNAM

... prides itself on well-presented food and uses lots and lots of fresh herbs and leaves – especially dill, lettuce, aromatic basil and fennel. Many foods (including *nem ran*, small spring rolls and morsels of meat or seafood) are eaten wrapped in fresh lettuce leaves with mint and coriander. The influences of French and Chinese cuisine are immediately apparent as is, to a lesser extent, the influence of Indian cooking in southern Vietnamese cooking. The colonial legacy has produced a uniquely delicate and fragrant cuisine.

> **... lots and lots of fresh herbs and leaves – especially dill, lettuce, aromatic basil and fennel ...**

Kowloon: Tsim Sha Tsui – Waterfront

The harbour-front, running around the southern tip of the Kowloon peninsula, offers some of the finest restaurants in Hong Kong – many of which are in Hong Kong's finest hotels. Others are in the expanse of shopping malls that stretches along Canton Road from the Ocean Terminal and Ocean Centre to Harbour City. Compared to the heart of Tsim Sha Tsui, this is the Riviera: affluent and delicious.

HARBOUR CITY

OCEAN TERMINAL

STAR FERRY

KOWLOON: TSIM SHA TSUI – WATERFRONT
Restaurants

Chesa ❶

1/F The Peninsula, Salisbury Rd, Tsim Sha Tsui, Kowloon

✆ 2315 3169

Ⓜ MTR (Tsim Sha Tsui Exit E)

Open: daily 1200–1500, 1830–2300

Reservations recommended

All credit cards accepted

Swiss

❷❸

The *fondues*, *raclettes*, dried *charcuteries* and other undeniably Swiss meals are exemplary; the *rösti* is the crispiest you'll taste. The Chesa, presented artfully as a delightful Alpine chalet, knows how to prepare filling food at its finest. Dangerous!

Felix ❶

28/F The Peninsula, Salisbury Rd, Tsim Sha Tsui, Kowloon

✆ 2315 3188

Ⓜ MTR (Tsim Sha Tsui Exit E)

Open: daily 1800–0200

Reservations essential

All credit cards accepted

Smart casual

International-Fusion

❷❸❹

From the moment the lift lights dim at the 28th floor you know you're in for a treat. This Philippe Starke-designed 'stage-set' is immediately entrancing. If you can't go for dinner, at least have a panoramic drink. The food, however, is every

bit as good as you'd hope, much of it French with a Japanese accent: the *teriyaki* quail on a goose liver pancake is ambrosial, and the seared sea bass on *wasabi* mash is a perfect combination. Delightfully decadent.

Gaddi's

The Peninsula, Salisbury Rd, Tsim Sha Tsui, Kowloon

✆ 2315 3171

Ⓜ MTR (Tsim Sha Tsui Exit E)

Open: daily 1200–1500, 1900–2300

Reservations recommended

All credit cards accepted

Jacket and tie required

French

💲💲💲

Formal and ornate, Gaddi's positively glistens with candelabras and chandeliers, and for decades has boasted some of the finest French food in town. Popular with romantic couples, business folk and food-lovers alike, traditional dishes are elegantly made modern. Dining here is special. Try the pan-fried turbot with asparagus and ceps mushrooms.

Imasa

1/F The Peninsula, Salisbury Rd, Tsim Sha Tsui, Kowloon

✆ 2315 3175

Ⓜ MTR (Tsim Sha Tsui Exit E)

Open: daily 1130–1430, 1800–2230

Reservations recommended

All credit cards accepted

Japanese

💲💲

Impressive Japanese food at reasonable prices, in a quiet, supremely tasteful, crisp and sophisticated setting. Exquisitely fresh sushi and *tempura* are prepared in front of you, and the *shabu shabu* and *sukiyaki* never disappoint. Private rooms available on request.

Lai Ching Heen Restaurant

L/G The Regent Hong Kong, 18 Salisbury Rd, Tsim Sha Tsui, Kowloon

▲ Felix

☎ 2721 1211 ext. 2243

🚇 MTR (Tsim Sha Tsui), Star Ferry Kowloon

Open: daily 1200–1430, 1800–2300

Reservations essential

All credit cards accepted

Jacket and tie

Cantonese

💲💲💲💲💲

Frequently billed as one of the best Chinese restaurants in Hong Kong since it opened in 1984, both the food and the décor (vast windows overlooking the harbour; jade and silver table-settings) are spectacular. The cooking is imaginative and artistic; try the deep-fried scallops with pears, and the roast duck with kiwi in lemon sauce. De luxe *dim sum* is available during the day. Honed to perfection.

Napa ❸

21/F The Kowloon Shangri-La, 64 Mody Rd, Tsim Sha Tsui East, Kowloon

☎ 2733 8752

🚇 MTR (Tsim Sha Tsui)

Reservations recommended

All credit cards accepted

American

💲💲

Stylish yet unpretentious, with a fresh, Navaho-inspired décor and panoramic views across the harbour. A modern west coast restaurant which uses ingredients to good effect – try the simple yet imaginative pasta in a chanterelle ragout, and Caesar salad in a parmesan basket. It's easy to spend more in the evening.

Ocean Palace Restaurant ❹

4/F Ocean Centre, Harbour City, Kowloon

☎ 2735 0866

🚇 Star Ferry Kowloon

Open: daily 0730–1630, 1800–2300

Reservations recommended

🔳 💳 American Express

Cantonese

💲

Surely one of the biggest and best-value restaurants in Hong Kong, brimming over with Chinese bustle. Try for a table near the vast inner stage for real atmosphere (it doubles as a nightclub sometimes). *Dim sum* is on the go all day, and the seafood is highly reputed. Try the fresh lobster steamed with ginger.

Plume ❷

G/F The Regent Hong Kong, 18 Salisbury Rd, Tsim Sha Tsui, Kowloon

☎ 2377 7888

🚇 MTR (Tsim Sha Tsui), Star Ferry Kowloon

Open: Mon–Sat 1800–2245

Reservations essential

All credit cards accepted

Jacket and tie

French

❸❸❸

French haute cuisine (with a little help from Continental neighbours), where herbs and the freshest, most luxurious ingredients are served in perfect symbiosis. Definitely for a special occasion, though the 'Twilight' set menu is excellent value.

The Royal Garden ❺

B/2 The Royal Garden Hotel, 69 Mody Rd, Tsim Sha Tsui East, Kowloon

☎ 2724 2666

🚇 MTR (Tsim Sha Tsui)

Open: daily 1130–1500, 1830–2300

Reservations recommended

All credit cards accepted

Cantonese

❸❸

A somewhat surreal entrance (with water fountain and bridge) leads into an ornate but classic restaurant. The roasted and minced pigeon is a speciality, and must be ordered in advance. Mainly Chinese clientele.

The Verandah ❶

1/F The Peninsula, Salisbury Rd, Tsim Sha Tsui, Kowloon

☎ 2315 3166

🚇 MTR (Tsim Sha Tsui Exit E)

Open: daily 1200–1500, 1830–2300

Reservations recommended

All credit cards accepted

International

❸❸

Rightly renowned for one of the most delicious buffet lunches – the ideal way to spend a lazy Sunday. You'll feel you've stepped back in time, and will be truly looked after by attentive staff, without the purse suffering too much.

Wan Loong Court ❻

Lower Level 2, The Kowloon Hotel, 19–21 Nathan Rd, Kowloon

☎ 2369 8698

🚇 MTR (Tsim Sha Tsui Exit E)

Open: Mon–Fri 1100–1500, 1800–2330, Sat–Sun 1100–2330

Reservations recommended

All credit cards accepted

Cantonese

❸❸

Owned by The Peninsula, the basement restaurant serves crisp, fresh and well-executed Chinese food. In the heart of tourist country, it is none the less enormously popular with local and visiting Chinese. An extensive *dim sum* menu is available all day on weekends … and the *har gau* (shrimp dumplings) are hard to beat. Eminently satisfying.

▲ Deep-fried scallops with pears, Lai Ching Heen Restaurant

KOWLOON: TSIM SHA TSUI – WATERFRONT
Bars, cafés and pubs

The Bar at The Peninsula ❶

1/F The Peninsula, Salisbury Rd, Tsim Sha Tsui, Kowloon

◉ MTR (Tsim Sha Tsui Exit E)

Open: daily 1130–2300

All credit cards accepted

A tranquil meeting place for a pre- or post-dinner drink. Quiet and elegant, The Bar evokes a privileged colonial feel and the chance to get away completely from the more hectic side of Hong Kong.

Dai Pai Dong ❼

G/F 66 Canton Rd, Tsim Sha Tsui, Kowloon

◉ MTR (Tsim Sha Tsui Exit A)

Open: Sun–Fri 0730–2400, Sat 0900–2400

No credit cards accepted

Part of a chain which preserves street-stall cooking, this is where you come for breakfast (*congee* – rice porridge), lunch (noodles) and dinner (more noodles). For those on a budget, this is excellent, filling and authentic. Photo menu available.

Happy Garden Noodle and Congee Kitchen ❽

76 Canton Rd, Tsim Sha Tsui, Kowloon

◉ MTR (Tsim Sha Tsui Exit A)

Open: daily 0700–0030

No credit cards accepted

A fine example of good-value Chinese eating, in a smartly polished rosewood interior; there are nearly 30 different types of *congee* (the scallop and shrimp balls are recommended). A true Cantonese experience.

Harbourside ❷

The Regent Hong Kong, 18 Salisbury Rd, Kowloon

◉ MTR (Tsim Sha Tsui), Star Ferry Kowloon

Open: daily 0800–2200

All credit cards accepted

For a decadent break, with stunning views across the harbour, the top-class Regent Hotel's coffee shop caters for international tastes, and does a special champagne brunch and children's buffet on Sundays. Casual but classy.

Maman wine bar and restaurant ❾

Regal Kowloon Hotel, 71 Mody Rd, Tsim Sha Tsui East, Kowloon

◉ MTR (Tsim Sha Tsui Exit D)

Open: Mon–Sat 1200–1430, 1800–2230

All credit cards accepted

For lovers of French wine, this ante-room to the Maman French restaurant boasts over 50 different wines by the glass, and is a wine oasis in this rather characterless part of TST East. Like a gentleman's club.

▲ Peninsula Lobby

Peninsula Lobby ❶

The Peninsula, Salisbury Rd, Tsim Sha Tsui, Kowloon

🚇 MTR (Tsim Sha Tsui Exit E)

Open: tea menu 1300–1700

All credit cards accepted

Tea at the Pen is compulsory! The ornate, gilded columns and piano accompaniment, are a perfect backdrop to an English tea with scones and finger sandwiches. Relaxing and fun – treat yourself.

Planet Hollywood ❿

3 Canton Rd, Harbour City, Tsim Sha Tsui, Kowloon

🚇 Star Ferry Kowloon

Open: daily 1130–0100 or later; happy hour 1730–1930 and after 2300

All credit cards accepted

Generally a grown-up's bar in the evening, yet loved by kids of all ages by day, the Planet has a very good value set lunch and menu comprising American food with an Asian twist.

Regent lounge lobby ❷

The Regent Hong Kong, 18 Salisbury Rd, Kowloon

🚇 MTR (Tsim Sha Tsui), Star Ferry Kowloon

Open: drinks 1100–2400

All credit cards accepted

Just the place to begin an evening in Kowloon: enjoy smart cocktails – on offer in a self-professed atmosphere of martini madness – in the hushed, slightly austere, art-deco style

HONG KONG

lobby of one of Hong Kong's top hotels.

Sushi bar ⓫

Basement 1, Silvercord Arcade, 30 Canton Rd, Tsim Sha Tsui, Kowloon

🚇 MTR (Tsim Sha Tsui Exit A)

Open: daily 1100–2230

All credit cards accepted

The Japanese fast food experience: select from over 50 kinds of sushi on a conveyor belt, and pay according to the colour of each plate. Order *miso* soup, pickled ginger or noodles separately. Sushi heaven for all the family.

Thousand Island Food Hall ⓬

Basement 2, Silvercord Arcade, 30 Canton Rd, Tsim Sha Tsui, Kowloon

🚇 MTR (Tsim Sha Tsui Exit A)

Open: daily 1100–2230

No credit cards accepted

The many counters in this arcade offer piping hot and very delicious food from all over Asia – from *sashimi*, Cantonese vegetarian, Indonesian *satay* and more. Packed with families. Ideal for a take-away in Kowloon Park.

Hong Kong Tourist Association

The branch at the Star Ferry concourse, on the Kowloon side, is an excellent place to gather up-to-date information about sites to see, tours to take, new restaurant openings, and so on. *Visitor hotline: 2508 1234. Open: Mon-Fri 0800–1800, Sat-Sun 0900–1700.*

KOWLOON: TSIM SHA TSUI – WATERFRONT
Shops, markets and picnic sites

Shops

City Super ⑬

Level 3 Harbour City
(adjacent to Prince Hotel)

🚢 Star Ferry Kowloon,
MTR (Tsim Sha Tsui)

Open: Sun–Thu 1030–2100,
Fri–Sat 1030–2200

All credit cards accepted

A supermarket-cum-delicatessen, with temptation and convenience in a single package. The fresh foods are beautifully presented, and include basic and speciality goods from several Asian countries. City Super has become something of a phenomenon in Hong Kong. Home deliveries are free of charge.

Délifrance ⑭

Basement, Hyatt Hotel,
67 Nathan Rd (entrance in
Peking Rd), Tsim Sha Tsui,
Kowloon

🚇 MTR (Tsim Sha Tsui)
Exit C)

Open: daily 0800–2100

No credit cards accepted

One in a large and successful chain, serving fairly standard baguette sandwiches, pastries and acceptable coffee. Seating is available.

Fine Foods ⑤

G/F The Royal Garden, 69
Mody Rd, Tsim Sha Tsui
East, Kowloon

🚇 MTR (Tsim Sha Tsui)
Exit D)

Open: Mon–Sat 0800–2000,
Sun 0700–2000

All credit cards accepted

A small but handy shop in TST East, selling freshly baked French breads and other *pâtisseries*, which also

sells wines and luxury chocolates.

Fortress 🔵

Shop 3320, 3/F Harbour City, Gateway II, Tsim Sha Tsui, Kowloon

🔵 Star Ferry Kowloon, MTR (Tsim Sha Tsui)

Open: Mon–Sat 0900–1900, Sun 1030–1800

All credit cards accepted

This large chain specialises in kitchen equipment and electrical goods – including a great selection of rice cookers. Another large branch is at: *Shop 3281, Level 3, Ocean Terminal, Tsim Sha Tsui.*

Marks & Spencer 🔵

Shops 102, 254 and 355, Levels 1–3 Ocean Centre, 5 Canton Rd, Tsim Sha Tsui, Kowloon

🔵 Star Ferry Kowloon, MTR (Tsim Sha Tsui)

Open: Mon–Sat 1000–1800

🔳 American Express

Although the food sections in Hong Kong's Marks & Spencer branches are minuscule (mainly selling biscuits and crisps), the wines are some of the least expensive and best value to be found in Hong Kong. There are branches in all of the main shopping areas.

Nam Pei Hong 🔵

3229 Harbour City, Tsim Sha Tsui, Kowloon

🔵 Star Ferry Kowloon, MTR (Tsim Sha Tsui)

Open: Mon–Sat 1000–1900, Sun 1100–1800

All credit cards accepted

Beautifully packaged for taking home, this is where you'll find all the speciality dried foods: not only Korean ginseng and Chinese mushrooms, but some of the items less common in a Western sense, such as dried caterpillars and *conpoy* (similar to scallops). Try the crispy dried squid strips, or baby whitebait, with your gin and tonic!

Oliver's Super Sandwiches 🔵

Shop 007, G/F Ocean Centre, Canton Rd, Tsim Sha Tsui

🔵 Star Ferry Kowloon, MTR (Tsim Sha Tsui)

Open: daily 1000–1800

All credit cards accepted

Part of a large chain selling freshly made sandwiches, pastries and breads, as well as general groceries and an extensive selection of wine and spirits. Some branches (though not this one) have seating areas.

Page One 🔵

Shop 3002, Harbour City, Tsim Sha Tsui, Kowloon

🔵 Star Ferry Kowloon, MTR (Tsim Sha Tsui)

Open: Sun–Thu 1030–2100, Fri–Sat 1030–2200

All credit cards accepted

An excellent cookery book section includes

several on Chinese and other Asian cuisines. There is also a good section on herbal and Chinese medicine.

Peninsula Boutique 🔵

Basement BE 7–9, East Wing, The Peninsula

🔵 MTR (Tsim Sha Tsui Exit E)

Open: daily 0930–1700

All credit cards accepted

For sinful cakes, Danish pastries and chocolates, or little luxuries to take home to friends, the Pen Boutique is hard to beat.

> Picnic sites

Waterfront Promenade 🔵

Southern tip of the Kowloon Peninsula, Tsim Sha Tsui, Kowloon

🔵 Star Ferry Kowloon

Turn right on disembarking from the Star Ferry, past the historic Clock Tower (44m high, built in 1915), and the Promenade offers a delightful stroll on a sunny day (although one can get rather windswept). For a close up of Hong Kong's busiest and most famous asset – its tremendous harbour – walk all the way along the harbour's edge, past the **Space Museum**, the **Museum of Art** and the Regent Hotel, towards the Kowloon-Canton Railway (KCR) terminus.

Rare and exotic

Balancing your body

If the body is at ease and in harmony with its environment, the mind will be able to deal with all changes in life.' So wrote Hui Si Hui in 1330, in *Yin Shan Zheng Yau*, the **Principles of Correct Diet**. An ideally balanced meal has five tastes (bitter, salt, sour, sweet and hot) to nurture the five vital organs (heart, kidneys, liver, spleen and lungs). Each food also has a specific role in maintaining or restoring health, balancing the *Ying* (female) and the *Yang* (male) forces, and increasing *qi*, or energy. Certain foods are outright nutritious, such as turtle jelly; some are invigorating or life-enhancing, such as ginseng; but others exert a more subtle influence, depending on their hot (or warming) or their cold (or cooling) qualities. Most spicy foods and most meats are hot or warming; most bitter foods are cold; and most salty foods, and some citrus, are cooling. Yet it seems there is no really easy way to identifying which foods are hot, cold, or the many warm, neutral and cool degrees in between: you just have to develop a feel for it!

And the system works! Obesity is still extremely rare in Hong Kong and China (in spite of the more recent efforts of Western fast-food chains). Since food plays such a crucial role, the **Cantonese** have become fairly adventurous in their cuisine. Indeed, nowadays, Cantonese food is notorious in its own right for incorporating almost anything, in a deep passion for good food and long life.

If your enthusiasm for the unusual doesn't quite extend to trying everything, perhaps the following insights may help to guide you in the right – or wrong – direction.

• **Snake:** if the Chinese-language menu at the **She Wong Yee** (*see page 41*) is too challenging, the snake soup at the **Sichuan Garden** simply has to be tried (*3/F Gloucester Tower, The Landmark, Central; ✆ 2521 4433; Ⓜ MTR (Central); open: daily 1130–1500, 1730–2330; reservations recommended; all credit cards accepted; Szechuan; ❸❸*). The snake is mixed with chicken stock, a little shredded chicken, finely sliced bamboo shoots and some cloud ear fungus, and the result is utterly delicious. Snake is seasonal.

• **Jellyfish** is the perfect ingredient in a cuisine which values texture (for texture's sake) as highly as Cantonese! Actually very innocuous to taste, it is commonly served in thin, ribbon-like slices and, if cooked well, is tender like good squid.

• **Eggs** are used far more imaginatively in Chinese cooking than in most Western cuisines. Salted eggs are popular snacks:

buried, salted eggs, including so-called 1000-year-old eggs (the earth-covered, black-and-white striped shells so striking in food markets), take on a rich and very sweet flavour. A must at any good Peking restaurant is the stir-fried dish of egg whites with shrimp or crabmeat, sprinkled with a little vinegar.

• **Black moss**, or *fa kai*, is also known as hair vegetable. Like many Cantonese delicacies, its taste is not strong at all, but its texture – slippery and slightly gelatinous, and with the capacity to absorb sauces like a light sponge – is most highly prized!

Unusual cuts of meat, such as **pig knuckle**, **brisket** and **ox's lung**, are a speciality of many snack shops and *dai pai dongs*. **Chung Kee** (*Food Court, Update Mall, 39 Nathan Rd, Tsim Sha Tsui, Kowloon;* ⊛ *MTR (Tsim Sha Tsui Exit E); open: daily 1100–2300; reservations not necessary; no credit cards accepted*) offers dishes such as **ox shoulder ligaments** (ideal if what you crave is an incredible chewing experience), and **ox penis**, to improve blood circulation. Civet cat, dog and bear's paw used to be favoured delicacies but are now illegal in Hong Kong.

• **Tortoise jelly** is made by brewing tortoise shell with ginseng and a complex concoction of over 20 other herbs. Served hot in small bowls, it is incredibly bitter – almost acrid – and eaten therefore with copious quantities of sugar. The

▲ 1000-year-old eggs

result promises to ease the circulation, help dermatitis, clear the system and generally 'relieve internal heat and dampness'.

• **Shark's fin** is sold dried; it requires hours of soaking and cooking to get exactly the right gelatinous texture – the quality for which it is so prized.

• **Bird's nest** is literally that: most prized are the nests of the golden shrikes which live in Hainan Province and near Borneo – the most dangerous and expensive to procure. Bird's nest is cooked in light chicken stock, and usually sweetened a little. The nest itself is quite tasteless but the birds' secretions and saliva are said to improve the complexion if taken over a period of time.

> **Bird's nest ... the birds' secretions and saliva are said to improve the complexion if taken over a period of time.**

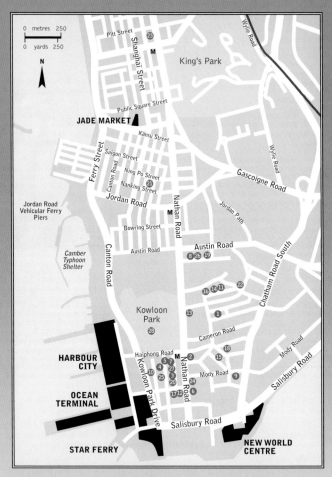

Kowloon: Tsim Sha Tsui, Yau Ma Tei and Mong Kok

The heart of Tsim Sha Tsui remains resolutely Chinese. This is a great area for eating royally yet cheaply, with a wealth of authentic Chinese regional restaurants and other tastes of Asia. Further north, Yau Ma Tei and Mong Kok have lots of new eateries amid the madly busy street life and night markets.

KOWLOON: TSIM SHA TSUI, YAU MA TEI AND MONG KOK
Restaurants

Au Trou Normand ❶

G and 1/F Taurus Bldg, 21A–B Granville Rd, Tsim Sha Tsui, Kowloon

✆ 2366 8754

🚇 MTR (Tsim Sha Tsui Exit E)

Open: daily 1200–1500, 1800–2300

Reservations recommended

All credit cards accepted

French

💲💲💲

With a long-standing reputation for fabulous, traditional French cuisine, this Hong Kong institution (now in its new home) never fails to please. It's possible to eat quite reasonably here – but you won't want to; the food is so good.

Banana Leaf Curry House ❷

3/F Golden Crown Court, 68 Nathan Rd, Tsim Sha Tsui, Kowloon

✆ 2721 4821

🚇 MTR (Tsim Sha Tsui Exit D)

Open: daily 1100–2400

Reservations unnecessary

All credit cards accepted

Malay

💲

One of the nicer branches of this chain, with good curries but rather banal, cafeteria-style décor. Take a window seat to watch hectic Nathan Road below. Malaysian, Singaporean and Thai curries, baked fish and other dishes are often served on banana leaves, with lovely fresh fruit juices.

Branto ❸

1/F 9 Lock Rd, Tsim Sha Tsui, Kowloon

✆ 2366 8171

🚇 MTR (Tsim Sha Tsui Exit C)

Open: daily 1100–1500, 1800–2300

Reservations recommended on Sat–Sun

💳 💳

Last orders 2230; takeaway available; not licensed

Indian-Vegetarian

💲

Billed rather bizarrely as a pizzeria and snack bar, the extensive menu is largely south Indian vegetarian. The restaurant is basic; it concentrates on the food, which is fabulous. Feast on fresh breads, *dosas* and Punjabi specialities at incredibly low prices. Very popular with the local Indian community.

Grand Hill ❹

37 Hankow Rd, Tsim Sha Tsui, Kowloon

✆ 2957 8883

🚇 MTR (Tsim Sha Tsui Exit C)

Open: daily 1130–0430

Reservations recommended

All credit cards accepted

Taiwanese

💲💲

Authentic, simple Taiwan cooking (where one can spot the Japanese influence in

▲ Tandoori sea bass

蕉葉咖喱屋
Banana Leaf Curry House

蕉葉集團網址 http://www.bananaleaf.com

flavour yet not at all in the presentation, which is less colourful and less artful). The Grand Hill has a very good hotpot menu and hotpot buffet. Staff are eager and helpful. It is often packed, and is popular for business lunches. Food is served into the small hours, but arrive before midnight.

Java Rijsttafel

G/F 38 Hankow Rd, Tsim Sha Tsui, Kowloon

☏ 2367 1230

🚇 MTR (Tsim Sha Tsui Exit C)

Open: daily 1200–2230

Reservations recommended

All credit cards accepted for bills above HK$200 only

Indonesian

💲

In this one small dining room, you can savour a medley of Indonesian, Malay and Singapore classics, including *satay*, *rendang* and *gado gado*, served by friendly hosts. All in all, this is a delightful place for lunch or dinner, and is popular, with fans prepared to queue in the tiny corridor outside; it

feels as though you're dining with friends.

The Khyber Pass

Block E, 7/F Chungking Mansions, 36–44 Nathan Rd, Tsim Sha Tsui, Kowloon

🚇 MTR (Tsim Sha Tsui Exit D)

Open: daily 1200–1530, 1800–2330

Reservations recommended for groups

No credit cards accepted

Indian

💲

Getting here is half the adventure. Hong Kongers have been braving the dodgy lift ascent for years. First find the Block E lifts, in the southeast corner of Chungking Mansions (film buffs will recognise the warren of shops on the ground floor of this building from *Chungking Express*). The dining room is basic, but the curries are good, and they cope admirably with large groups. An experience.

Macau Restaurant ⑦

27 Lock Rd, Tsim Sha Tsui, Kowloon

☏ 2366 8148

🚇 MTR (Tsim Sha Tsui Exit C1)

Open: daily 0700–0200

Reservations difficult; be prepared to queue

No credit cards accepted

Macanese

💲

A basic, chaotic, cafeteria-style venue – but with queues that testify to the excellence and authenticity of the food, from grilled Portuguese *sardinhas* and *bacalhau* (salted cod fish) to cuttlefish with soy and green onions. Another branch has now opened in Granville Road.

Shabu Shabu ⑧

G/F 3 Hillwood Rd, Tsim Sha Tsui, Kowloon

☏ 2314 4292

🚇 MTR (Tsim Sha Tsui Exit B)

Open: daily 1800–0200

Reservations recommended

All credit cards accepted

Japanese

💲💲

A very extensive menu is available, but this restaurant specialises in its namesake hotpot dish – which you cook at your own table or at a bar counter. Even if you usually shy away from set meals, you are well advised to try it here, as it combines all the best dishes. Sublime eel!

Spring Deer ⑨

1/F 42 Mody Road, Tsim Sha Tsui, Kowloon

☏ 2366 4012

MTR (Tsim Sha Tsui
Exit D)

Open: daily 1200–1500,
1800–2300 (last orders
2230)

Reservations essential

No credit cards accepted

Peking

⑤

This long-established
favourite claims to serve
'the best Peking food' –
and it does! Ask for
shredded beef in chilli
sauce, which you eat in
little pockets of sesame
bread, or sweet chilli
prawns. Definitely try
the scrambled egg white
with crabmeat – served
with a little vinegar, it
is hard to believe how
seriously yummy this is!
If you want Beggar's
Chicken, order it the
day before. The entrance
is well hidden so keep
your eye out for the
large neon street sign.

Star Café ⑩

21A Ashley Rd, Tsim Sha
Tsui, Kowloon

℘ 2736 1722

MTR (Tsim Sha Tsui
Exit A)

Open: daily 1130–1500,
1800–2230

Reservations essential

▨ ▧

International

⑤

This place has come to
enjoy incredible popu-
larity for the sheer good
value of its food.
Expect the place to be
packed out.
International dishes,
such as French *escargot*
and New Zealand lamb,

range from reliable to
delicious.

Tutto Bene ⑪

7 Knutsford Terrace, Tsim
Sha Tsui, Kowloon

℘ 2316 2116

MTR (Tsim Sha Tsui
Exit C)

Reservations recommended

All credit cards accepted

Italian

⑤⑤

A smart-casual Italian
restaurant in the area
which some have billed
as the up-and-coming
rival to trendy Soho on
Hong Kong Island. The
hearty and innovative
pasta dishes are

recommended – as is
alfresco dining on a
spring evening!

Wu Kong Shanghai Restaurant ⑫

Alpha House Basement,
27–33 Nathan Rd (entrance
in Peking Rd), Tsim Sha
Tsui, Kowloon

℘ 2366 7244

MTR (Tsim Sha Tsui
Exit E)

Open: 1130–2400

Reservations recommended

All credit cards accepted

Shanghai

⑤⑤

Highly thought of by
many Hong Kong
Chinese, this is a great

place to try Shanghai-style *dim sum* (the photo-menu is very handy!). Try a Chinese Shaoxing yellow wine with your braised yellow fish with sweet-sour sauce.

Xi 🕦

Arcade 2, Miramar Hotel, 118–30 Nathan Rd, Tsim Sha Tsui, Kowloon

🚇 MTR (Tsim Sha Tsui Exit B)

Open: daily 1200–1430, 1830–2230

Reservations recommended

All credit cards accepted

International

💲💲💲

A sister restaurant to Cantonese-serving **Dong** next door, Xi serves Western food with an Oriental spin, in smart, chic surroundings. Seafood is guaranteed fresh, and the West-meets-East desserts are a great success.

KOWLOON: TSIM SHA TSUI, YAU MA TEI AND MONG KOK
Bars, cafés and pubs

Bahama Mamas 14

4–5 Knutsford Terrace, Tsim Sha Tsui, Kowloon

🅜 MTR (Tsim Sha Tsui Exit C)

Open: Mon–Fri 1500–0300, Sat 1700–0400, Sun 1800–0200

VISA 💳 American Express

Bahama Mamas has created a laid-back Caribbean feel, ideal for a tropical cocktail to start the evening off, or a late-night drink when things really get going. The bar is spacious or you can enjoy drinks al fresco on the terrace (though the view is of several hundred Hong Kong air-conditioners), and a table football makes the place fun.

Biergarten 15

5 Hanoi Rd, Tsim Sha Tsui, Kowloon

🅜 MTR (Tsim Sha Tsui Exit D)

Open: daily 1200–0100 or later

All credit cards accepted

Specialising in imported German draught and bottled beers, this busy and friendly pub also serves a simple but good range of German bar food.

Chasers 16

G/F Carlton Bldg, 2–3 Knutsford Terrace, Tsim Sha Tsui, Kowloon

🅜 MTR (Tsim Sha Tsui Exit B)

Open: Mon–Fri 1600–0400, Sat–Sun 1200–0400

All credit cards accepted

Just along from Bahama Mamas, Chasers strongly resembles an English pub and attracts a mixed clientele. It serves Western bar snacks, and different visiting bands play rock and pop music later on in the evening, for night owls.

Delaneys 17

Basement, Mary Building, 71–7 Peking Rd, Tsim Sha Tsui, Kowloon

🅜 MTR (Tsim Sha Tsui Exit C1)

Open: daily 1100–0200

All credit cards accepted

This determinedly Irish pub is welcoming, convivial and relaxed, with Irish beers its speciality. A selection of Irish sporting memorabilia betrays its patriotism – if you were in any doubt! The bar food, especially the set lunch, is very good value. Extremely popular with locals, expatriates and visitors alike, and one can see why.

The Oxford Circus 18

3–7A Prat Ave., Tsim Sha Tsui, Kowloon

🅜 MTR (Tsim Sha Tsui Exit A/D)

Open: daily 1030–0230

All credit cards accepted

A friendly British pub with a large and faithful local clientele, a good place to meet for pre-dinner drinks, or just to while away an evening with friends. Good and sustaining bar food. The music gets louder as the evening wears on and there is dancing at the weekends.

Restaurant da Praia Grande 19

23 Hillwood Rd, Tsim Sha Tsui, Kowloon

🅜 MTR (Tsim Sha Tsui Exit B)

Open: daily 1200–2300

VISA 💳

A Macanese restaurant that serves afternoon tea of re-energising proportions and good (Italian) coffee. Popular among local Chinese, you could do worse than stay on for an authentic Macanese supper – Portuguese with an undeniable and underpinning Asian spin.

▲ Temple Street Market food stalls

Shadowman Cyber Café ⑳

G/F Karlock Bldg, 7 Lock Rd, Tsim Sha Tsui, Kowloon

🚇 MTR (Tsim Sha Tsui Exit C)

Open: daily 0830–0030

No credit cards accepted

A cosy cyber café where a food or drink purchase buys you 20 minutes of free internet surfing. Good coffees, salads and burgers are on offer. Industrious yet relaxed.

Temple Street Market food stalls ㉑

Temple St and Kansu St, Tsim Sha Tsui, Kowloon

🚇 MTR (Jordan Exit C)

Open: daily 0800–2300

No credit cards accepted

The market (cheap 'designer' clothing, watches, wallets, and so on) really takes off in the evening. Take your pick of any of the seafood, clay pot and noodle cafés lining Nanking and Nin Po Streets. Alternatively, for a slightly more relaxed environment, head for the large café enclosure at the corner of Temple Street and Hoi Street, where you can watch your meal being prepared. Most of the establishments here have an English-language menu, and serve beer and soft drinks.

Wild Poppies Café and Bar ㉒

G/F 65A Kimberley Rd, Tsim Sha Tsui, Kowloon

🚇 MTR (Tsim Sha Tsui Exit B)

Open: Mon–Sat 1200–0100, Sun 1500–0100

No credit cards accepted

Unpretentious and friendly café serving simple, mainly Italian snacks with an Asian twist, teas and coffees. Licensed.

Yee Shun Milk Company ㉓

519 Nathan Rd, Yau Ma Tei, Kowloon

🚇 MTR (Yau Ma Tei Exit B)

Open: daily 0800–2330

No credit cards accepted

A Chinese milkshake bar! Refreshing papaya or coconut milk drinks; yummy steamed milk with ginger juice; little bowls of sweet milk desserts. A haven for the sweet-toothed.

Shops

Delicatessen Corner 24

Basement 1, Holiday Inn Golden Mile, 50 Nathan Rd, Tsim Sha Tsui

Ⓜ MTR (Tsim Sha Tsui Exit D)

Open: daily 0800–2400, takeaway counter 0730–2400

All credit cards accepted

Actually a German restaurant, with hearty dishes and open-faced sandwiches; but the takeaway counter here is also tempting, with cheeses, meats, chocolates and even Chinese festival cakes at the right times of the year.

Kee Wah cake shop 25

25 Hankow Rd, Tsim Sha Tsui, Kowloon

Ⓜ MTR (Tsim Sha Tsui Exit A)

Open: daily 0800–2000

■■ ➔ American Express

An array of savoury buns, and the signature cakes: sweet *Ka Nui Beng*, which are moulded shortcakes with centres of walnut, lotus seed and egg yolk, red bean, coconut,

pumpkin, melon, mango, and so on.

Siver Bell Fine Wines and Spirits 26

6 Hillwood Rd, Tsim Sha Tsui, Kowloon

Ⓜ MTR (Tsim Sha Tsui Exit B)

Open: Mon–Sat 1100–2100, Sun 1300–1900

All credit cards accepted

With a wide selection of Old and New World wines, including a good range of half-bottles; there is another branch at 178 Nathan Road.

Swindon Book Company Ltd 27

13–15 Lock Rd, Tsim Sha Tsui, Kowloon

Ⓜ MTR (Tsim Sha Tsui Exit C1)

Open: Mon–Sat 1000–1800

All credit cards accepted

One of the larger and older bookstores in this established company, with a section on cookery and Chinese herbal medicines.

Picnic sites

Kowloon Park 28

Bounded by Haiphong Rd, Nathan Rd and Austin Rd

Ⓜ MTR (Tsim Sha Tsui Exit A)

Heavily landscaped with fountains, sculptures, a chess garden and paved walkways, but none the less a haven of peace and tranquillity. The park includes an exotic aviary – and several rare birds fly free yet call the park home. Alongside is Kowloon's busiest street, Nathan Road, named after the Governor who widened it (amid much ridicule, since the area was then so sparsely populated) in 1907.

▲ Shark's fins

Yam sing!

Chinese wines and spirits

Odds are that you will be able to find virtually any drink you desire in the gastronomic city of Hong Kong, and odds are, if you have Western tastes, that you may stick to local beers or imported wines. Yet there is a huge variety of Chinese wines and spirits there for the tasting. As with many things in Hong Kong, drinking can involve an etiquette which is mysteriously bound up with status, prestige, health and happiness.

Whereas tea rightly deserves the title of national drink, the often hot and humid climate encourages a fair amount of **beer** consumption too! Three popular lagers are brewed locally: **Carlsberg**, **San Miguel**, and the slightly more fragrant **Tsingtao** –

▲ Wines in a supermarket

the latter is still brewed in China according to a 1930s German recipe. Other Asian beers such as **Tiger Beer**, brewed in Singapore, and **Sappuro**, from Japan, are also available fairly widely. In fact, lager complements Cantonese, Thai and Indian food particularly well.

When it comes to imported **wines and spirits**, Hong Kong is a prime consumer. A few decades ago, more XO and VSOP **cognac** was drunk in Hong Kong than in France. Nowadays, in spite of the cost (imported wine can easily make up half of your bill in a top restaurant), a fashion and a passion for wine drinking have developed. Particularly popular and prestigious are famous **European vintages**, especially the classic French *Grands Crus* of **Bordeaux**.

Which imported wines to drink with which cuisines? Rich cooking from Beijing, Szechuan or Hunan is nicely complemented by strong, rich, flavoursome red wines, say from **California**, **Chile**, **Australia** or the **Rhône Valley**. Lighter red wines, such as a **Beaujolais** or Italian **Barbera**, suit Shanghai cooking, which tends to be a little oilier. Cantonese cuisine, with its subtler flavours, is ideally matched with a dry minerally white wine, such as a **Chablis**; whereas fragrant and floral grapes, such as the **Gewürztraminer** and **Tokay Pinot**

Gris in Alsace wines, are a perfect partner for most Thai food. If in doubt, a light, dry Italian **Pinot Grigio** is always good to accompany Asian dishes.

But for a more authentic adventure, uncork the local wine! **'Jiu'** are Chinese alcoholic beverages, and most Chinese alcohol is distilled from rice and other cereals, sometimes with flowers, herbs and other added ingredients. The wines and spirits tend to be sweet and aromatic, often flavoured with plants such as green bamboo leaves, papaya and lotus flowers. A fiery, spicy Szechuan meal is an excellent opportunity to try one or two! **Shaoxing** (or yellow wine) is a liquor produced in Zhejiang province; different grades are available (in ever more ornate and decorative bottles) and the more mature the better. It is drunk warm, and is mellow and supple. Not only an ideal partner to Chinese food, it is also used to marinate drunken chicken. A much stronger and harsher, but equally well known, Chinese spirit is **'maotai'**, made from millet. *Maotai*, the Chinese equivalent of Russia's vodka or Italy's grappa, is often the spirit of choice for *yam sing*, or *gan bei* (bottoms up) toasts at banquets or large meals ... and has a completely deserved reputation therefore for being particularly lethal! **'Kao ling'** and **'sui hing'**, are almost as powerful and, like *maotai*, available in most supermarkets; they are often served as winter warmers.

Reassuringly, many Chinese spirits are good for you! Ingredients are added to a range of liquors, all for the betterment of one's health. For example, **'san she jiu'** (snake wine) combines the beneficial effects from soaking three different snakes in rice wine: the Chinese cobra, the banded krait and the elaphe radiata. The resultant concoction not only stimulates blood circulation and strengthens bones and tendons but also, if taken frequently, will cause muscles and joints to relax. Other wines, for example, flavoured with ginseng and ginger, have fortifying and **aphrodisiac properties**.

Intriguingly, China has been producing **grape wine** for a long time (in vineyards spread north of the Yangtse River) but has yet to earn a strong following. The two most easily available labels are **Great Wall** and **Dynasty**: the reds are light and quite sweet; the whites resemble German Hock. Recently, large New World and European companies have invested in Chinese vineyards, so it seems only a matter of time before the vast and varied soils and climates of China reap some truly high-quality wines from the many indigenous grape varieties available.

> **Ingredients are added to a range of liquors, all for the betterment of one's health.**

The New Territories and outlying islands

The New Territories and outlying islands are easier to reach than you might think – and represent the true essence of Hong Kong. As Ying balances Yang, the remoter parts offer breathtaking scenery while many of the 'new towns' have malls to rival those of Causeway Bay and Tsim Sha Tsui.

Lau Fau S
Tin Sh
Ha Ts
Lung Kwu
Sheung Tan
Tai
Ma Wan Chung
Lantau Islan
Tai O
⑪ Ngong Pin
⑥
⑩ Ch
Shek Pik
Soko Islands

THE NEW TERRITORIES AND OUTLYING ISLANDS
Restaurants

New Territories

Cosmopolitan Curry House ①

80 Kwong Fuk Rd, Tai Po Market, Tai Po

✆ 2650 7056

🚇 KCR to Tai Po Market

Open: daily 1100–2330

Reservations essential

💳 💳 💳

Indonesian-Malay

$ $

Hong Kong residents speak lovingly of superb meals at this simple but usually packed restaurant. Many of the dishes blend sweet and spicy, such as the delectable prawn and mango curry.

Firenzi Ristorante ②

G/F 60 Po Tung Rd, Sai Kung

✆ 2792 0898

🚇 MTR (Diamond Hill) and bus 92, or MTR (Choi Hung) and minibus 1A

Open: daily 1130–2230 (last orders)

Reservations recommended at weekends

💳 💳 American Express

Italian

$ $

Immensely popular with the Chinese and Western residents of Sai Kung, the pasta here is cooked to perfection. Just what you need after a day trekking through the Sai Kung Country Park.

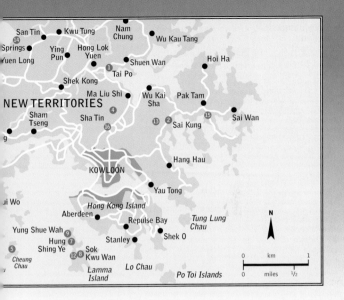

San Tin • • Kwu Tung   Nam
                        Chung • • Wu Kau Tang
Springs • 14
         Ying   Hong Lok   Hoi Ha •
Yuen Long Pun   Yuen
                   • Shuen Wan
           Hong Lok
              1
          Shek Kong Tai Po
uen Long   Ma Liu Shi • Wu Kai Pak Tam
NEW TERRITORIES   Sha
     Sham   Sha Tin   4   15
     Tseng   13   Sai Wan •
g •   16   Sai Kung 2
                            • Sai Kung

              KOWLOON
                        • Hang Hau

ui Wo   • Yau Tong
      Hong Kong Island
   Aberdeen •   • Repulse Bay Tung Lung
Yung Shue Wah 9   Chau
    Hung 7   Stanley • • Shek O
5 Shing Ye 8 Sok
         12 Kwu Wan
Cheung   Lama   Lo Chau   Po Toi Islands
Chau   Island

                    N

          0   km   1
          0   miles   1/2

▲ Tai O, Lantau Island

Golden Bangkok Thai Food Restaurant ③

G/F Flat AB Win Hing Ct, Shui Chi Kwun St, Yuen Long

✆ 2470 0273

🚇 None – take a taxi

Open: daily 1200–1430, 1800–2200

Reservations unnecessary

No credit cards accepted

Thai

💲

A fairly basic establishment which serves wonderful, authentic Thai dishes. The minced pork with chillies and basil is hot, and the tender squid yellow curry and baked rice in a whole coconut sublime.

Ming Yuen Seafood Restaurant ②

G/F 78–81 Man Nin St, Sai Kung

✆ 2792 2228

🚇 MTR (Diamond Hill) and bus 92, or MTR (Choi Hung) and minibus 1A

Open: daily 1100–2230

Reservations unnecessary

No credit cards accepted

Chinese-Seafood

💲

The fresh local seafood dishes include the intriguingly described yet extremely tasty stewed barnacle with strong wine, and the lobster in superior soup.

四川樓

天府風味

電話：二八九一九○二七

香港銅鑼灣渣甸道四六號

Pepperoni ②

1592 Po Tung Rd, Sai Kung

✆ 2792 2083

🚇 MTR (Diamond Hill) and bus 92, or MTR (Choi Hung) and minibus 1A

Open: daily 1000–2330

Reservations recommended evenings

American Express

Takeaway available

Italian

💲💲

Now with branches in Soho and Wanchai, Pepperoni is immensely popular (and diners often face something of a wait). Great value pizzas and pastas arrive in enormous portions, and Sai Kung residents say they couldn't live without it!

Shatin Inn ④

7-and-a-half miles, Tai Po Rd, Sha Tin

✆ 2691 1425

🚇 None – take KCR to Tai Wai, then a taxi

Open: daily 1200–2330

Reservations unnecessary

No credit cards accepted

Takeaway available

Indonesian

💲

Ideal for a lazy autumn afternoon, or to relax up in the hills after a day at the Shatin Races. Delicious Indonesian dishes (including speciality meat and seafood *satay*) are served by friendly staff. For alfresco diners, food is

kept warm on tabletop charcoal burners. Children and groups welcomed.

Outlying islands

Baccarat ⑤

G/F 9A Pak She Praya Rd, Cheung Chau Island

✆ 2981 0668

⛴ Ferry (Pier No 6) from Central

Open: daily 1100–2330

Reservations unnecessary

VISA 💳

Takeaway available

Chinese-Seafood

💲

Locals rave about this place, not only for its freshly cooked (and freshly caught) seafood, but also for its location by the harbour's edge. There is a good English-language menu.

Good View Seafood Restaurant ⑥

15 Wing On St, Tai O, Lantau Island

✆ None available

⛴ Ferry from Central to Mui Wo (Silvermine Bay), bus to Tai O

Open: daily 0800–2200

Reservations unnecessary

No credit cards accepted

Chinese-Seafood

💲

Standard seafood dishes and huge mountains of *chow faan* (fried rice) adorn every table. The baked crab with green onions and ginger is good; Westerners tend not to opt for the soft-shell turtle.

Hong Kee Restaurant ❺

G/F 11A Pak She Praya Rd, Cheung Chau Island

✆ 2981 9916

🚢 Ferry (Pier No 6) from Central

Open: daily 1100–2400

Reservations unnecessary

No credit cards accepted

Chinese-Seafood

$

Many of the seafood restaurants on Cheung Chau are good, but here they do something wonderful to the shrimp. Even the scrambled eggs with shrimp are delicious.

Hon Lok Yuen (aka 'The Pigeon Restaurant') ❼

16 Hung Shing Ye, Yung Shue Wan, Lamma Island

✆ 2982 0608/0680

🚢 Ferry (Pier No 5) from Central

Open: daily 1200–2230

Reservations essential – telephone to specify number of people and pigeons

No credit cards accepted

Open air

Chinese

$

A 15-minute walk from Yung Shue Wan ferry pier, it's best to take a torch and pick a warm (the restaurant is open air), moonlit evening. Opt for (and specify when you book) the unbelievably delicious minced pigeon, served with pinenuts and herbs, eaten in lettuce leaves with *hoi sin* sauce.

Lamma Mandarin Seafood Restaurant ❽

G/C 8 First St, Sok Kwu Wan, Lamma Island

✆ 2982 8128

🚢 Ferry (Pier No 5) from Central

Open: daily 1200–2300

Reservations recommended for groups and weekends

VISA 💳

Chinese-Seafood

$

You absolutely must try the deep-fried squid, served at most of the neighbouring establishments yet somehow that touch crispier and that little bit more tender here.

Lamma Seaview Man Fung Seafood Restaurant ❾

5 Main St, Yung Shue Wan, Lamma Island

✆ 2892 1112

🚢 Ferry (Pier No 5) from Central

Open: daily 1100–2200

Reservations recommended for large groups and weekends

VISA 💳 American Express

Chinese-Seafood

$

Among the succulent seafood dishes at the Man Fung is its famous, creamy crab with plum sauce. Of the many seafood restaurants at Yung Shue Wan, the Man Fung is a HKTA member.

Lancombe Seafood Restaurant ❾

G/F 47 Main St, Yung Shue Wan, Lamma Island

✆ 2982 0881

🚢 Ferry (Pier No 5) from Central

Open: daily 1100–2230

Reservations recommended for groups and weekends

VISA 💳 American Express

Chinese-Seafood

$

The Lancombe is also famous for its crab dishes, and has great

▲ Good View Seafood Restaurant

▲ Po Lin Buddhist Monastery

views across the busy (in a sleepy, Lamma Island sort of way) waterfront.

Lower Cheung Sha Beach 🔟

Nr Tong Fuk Village, Lower Cheung Sha, Lantau Island

✆ None available

🚢 Ferry from Central to Mui Wo (Silvermine Bay) and bus to Cheung Sha/Po Lin

Open: daily 1200–1500, 1730–2100

Reservations unnecessary

No credit cards accepted

Chinese

💲

After a visit to Po Lin, stroll on the long sandy beach at sunset, and stop off at either of the two restaurants here – both favourites of Hong Kong expatriates, who rave about the salt-and-pepper squid.

Peach Garden Seafood Restaurant 🅼

DD10, Lot 583 Sok Kwu Wan, Lamma Island

✆ 2982 8581

🚢 Ferry (Pier No 5) from Central

Open: daily 1200–2200

Reservations recommended for large groups

💳 American Express

Chinese-Seafood

💲

In a quieter location than most of the Sok Kwu Wan restaurants, this is a short stroll in the opposite direction – perhaps as good a reason as any for its popularity. Try the shrimps with black pepper sauce, chilli and garlic: pure heaven.

Po Lin vegetarian restaurant 🕚

Po Lin Buddhist Monastery, Lantau Island

✆ 2985 5113

🚢 Ferry from Central to Mui Wo (Silvermine Bay), bus to Po Lin

Open: daily 1130–1700

Reservations recommended for large groups

💳

Vegetarian

💲

Visitors to the upper levels of the magnificent, 26m-high bronze statue of Buddha are entitled to a free meal with the same ticket. The food is tasteful and sustaining, though the busy restaurant surroundings are hardly serene.

Rainbow Seafood Restaurant 🅼

16–20 First St, Sok Kwu Wan, Lamma Island

✆ 2982 8100

🚢 Ferry (Pier No 5) from Central

Open: daily 1200–2300

Reservations recommended for groups and weekends

💳 American Express

Chinese-Seafood

💲

A HKTA member, the Rainbow entices custom by running its own boat service (call for details). Relish a simply steamed fish, Cantonese style, or the dreamy baked lobster with butter for which the restaurant is so well known.

THE NEW TERRITORIES AND OUTLYING ISLANDS
Shops, markets and picnic sites

Markets

Cheung Chau Market 5

Cheung Chau Island

🅟 Ferry (Pier No 6) from Central

No credit cards accepted

Straight ahead from the ferry pier, the market offers all the sounds and sights (some of them quite gruesome) of a culture that prizes fresh food so highly. Don't be surprised to see frogs being skinned alive, or turtles ready for the chop. None the less, if time is short, this is food culture in microcosm.

Tai O Market 6

Tai O Wing On St and Kat Hing St, Tai O, Lantau

🅟 Ferry to Mui Wo (Silvermine Bay) Lantau Island and bus 1 to Tai O Market

No credit cards accepted

A unique fishing community, still hanging on to tradition in spite of creeping modernisation, its homes are an extraordinary clutter of boats and platforms on stilts. The ancient Tanka settlement was founded on fish farming and salt panning, and today

Tai O is still famous for its many dried fish and other seafood shops. Its particular speciality is fish paste, a pungent, pink substance sold in jars, and to be seen (and smelled!) drying on large flat baskets around the village.

Picnic sites

Cheung Sha Beach 10

Cheung Sha, Lantau Island

🅟 Ferry from Central to Mui Wo, bus to Cheung Sha

The longest beach and best swimming area on southern Lantau, with convenient refreshment shops and restaurants nearby.

Hung Shing Ye Beach 7

Hung Shing Ye, Lamma Island

🅟 Ferry to Yung Shue Wan from Hong Kong

One of the three main recreational beaches on Lamma, reached by path from the main village of Yung Shue Wan (with its main street lined with pubs, cafés and shops, as well as a temple to the goddess Tin Hau).

Lo So Shing Beach 12

Lo So Shing, Lamma Island

🅟 Ferry to Sok Kwu Wan from Hong Kong

One of the three main beaches, reached by cutting across Lamma from Sok Kwu Wan, after passing the long line of open-air seafood restaurants, and the Tin Hau Temple (about 150 years old, with a charming part-of-the-furniture dusty feel to it).

Maclehose Trail 13

From Sai Kung to Tuen Mun, beginning at Tsak Yue Wu, Sai Kung East Country Park, New Territories

🅟 To Sai Kung by MTR (Diamond Hill) and bus 92, or MTR (Choi Hung) and minibus 1A; then minibus from Sai Kung to Pak Tam Chung

A 100km route carved out of the hills for walkers and nature-lovers. The four reservoirs and varied scrubland provide habitats for all manner of birdlife, butterflies, macaque monkeys and abundant shrubs – including the orange-red *Lantana* that so typifies wild Hong Kong. The route is divided into ten sections for convenience.

▲ Cheung Sha Beach

Mai Po Marshes and Nature Reserve ⑭

World Wide Fund for Nature (Hong Kong), Mai Po, New Territories

🚇 None – take advice when you book

Open: three-hour sessions every half hour, Sat–Sun from 0900–1500

Reservations essential

The WWF Office is at 1 Tramway Path, Central (✆ 2526 1011).

Actually a world-famous bird sanctuary, managed by the World Wildlife Fund. Public visits are guided and include walking around these magical marsh-lands – a truly memo-rable experience – and a visit to the Captive Waterflow Collection.

Po Lin Monastery ⑪

Po Lin, Lantau Island

🚇 Ferry to Mui Wo (Silvermine Bay) Lantau, bus to Po Lin

After conquering the 268 steps up to the largest statue of Buddha in East Asia, and admir-ing Lantau's Ngong Ping plateau, the Po Lin gardens offer well-earned respite. Po Lin (literally 'precious lotus') was established as a retreat in 1920.

 Sha Tin KCR Station, across the Shing Mun River along Sha Tin Rural Committee Rd, to Sha Kok Rd; follow signs for Jat Min Shuen

One of Hong Kong's older 'new towns', Sha Tin houses over 750,000 people in its soaring tower blocks, and each week during the racing season thousands of race-goers visit the Jockey Club's second horse-racing track here. Vestiges of older Hong Kong culture can still be found: a traditional walled village lies to the south of Sha Tin station. This is Tsang Tai Uk, fortified in the 19th century and still home to the Tsang clan.

Tung Wan Beach ❺

Cheung Chau Beach Rd, Cheung Chau Island

🅟 Ferry (Pier No 6) from Central

A tiny (c. 2.5 sq. km) island, Cheung Chau is quite densely populated (about 40,000 people) yet its pace is somehow slower, and its lifestyle more traditional. Tung Wan beach, on the opposite side to the ferry pier, is the most popular swimming area and picnic spot. Culture-hounds might be interested in the Bronze Age rock carving at the southern end of the beach, or the Pak Tai Temple, built in 1783, on Pak She St near the northern end of the beach.

Sheung Yiu Folk Museum ⓯

Sheung Yiu village, Sai Kung Country Park, New Territories

🅟 MTR (Diamond Hill) and bus 92, or MTR (Choi Hung) and minibus 1A to Sai Kung

A clearly signposted 'culture trail' leads to a terrace of 200-year-old restored village houses, containing artefacts, agricultural implements and costumes from long-lost Chinese village culture. Ready-made barbecue pits are dotted along the route. Just past the Sheung Yiu Museum, the route leads to a Tang Dynasty (10th century AD) lime kiln.

Tsang Tai Uk ⓰

Sha Kok Rd, Sha Tin

Festival foods

Time-honoured customs

Even modern Hong Kong nurtures its ancient customs and every roadside shrine or flamboyant festival is a reminder of how food is inextricably linked to religion. In fact, food is as important to the health of the dead as to the living. It is believed that when you die, your soul continues to live on sacrificial offerings until, finally, it goes peacefully and nourished to the underworld. This is ancestor worship – time-honoured customs relating to health, status, wealth and happiness, which underpin the more formal strictures of Taoism, Buddhism and Confucianism.

A spirit ancestor (*tso sin*) with no family to care for it becomes a hungry ghost – a *kwai*. The *Yue Lan* or **Hungry Ghosts Festival** (Day 15 of Moon 7), when the doors of the underworld open, is therefore a worrying time! Serious effort is required to placate the ghosts; symbols of wealth are burned and food, such as noodle

▲ Moon cakes

mountains and decorated fruits, is displayed in magnificent if gaudy ceremony in matshed theatres throughout Hong Kong ... all under the watchful eye of Taai Si Wong, the spirit recorder who reports all to Heaven's omni-potent Jade Emperor.

Ancestor worship, like **feng shui** and **fortune telling**, is very much concerned with matters of prestige and status, or 'face'. Daily offerings honour the oldest of the Chinese gods, shamans who live in the earth, trees, water and even the home. The New Territories and urban streets alike are filled with shrines to these gods. In town, it is the Kitchen God who safe-guards households and reports at the end of each year to the Jade Emperor. On **New Year's Eve**, a special offering is made of rice with honey and sticky syrup – to make the Kitchen God's report sweet and flattering!

Another spectacular event is Cheung Chau Island's **Bun (Tai Chiu) Festival**, usually held in May – though the precise date is decided annually by divination. Huge mountains of sweet buns are paraded through the streets to the island's famous Pak Tai Temple, both to worship ancestors and to commemorate Pak Tai's help in quelling a terrible plague epidemic about 100 years ago. Until recently, the bun mountains carried a small child on top, and at the end of the parade an unceremonious scramble took place to grab the buns, though near-accidents have since rewritten these rules with rather more decorum.

Come September, at the **Mid-Autumn or 'Moon Festival'** (Day 15 of Moon 8), Hong Kong lights up. People gather in parks and high places as the moon rises, with colourful, candlelit paper lanterns in all shapes and sizes, and munch on 'moon cakes' (*yuek beng*), made from ground sesame and lotus seed using wooden paddles rather like English butter pats. Moon Festival actually celebrates an uprising against the Mongols in the 14th century, when the call to arms was written on slips of paper baked into the cakes; today, the messages herald fortune and longevity.

New Year (January/February) is the time for clearing debts and ushering in the new, with wishes for good fortune and a long life … and the entire event seems to revolve around food! On New Year's Eve the table is set for the whole family – including spirit ancestors – and 'gold ingots' (dumplings) and *warm family reunion* (stuffed duck and pickled eggs) are among the special dishes. New Year's Day features equally auspicious-sounding dishes, such as 'profitable coming years' (fish and lotus seed in garlic sauce) and, of course, special, glutinous baked puddings made with coconut, or sweet turnip, or *conpoy*, whose Chinese

> **Serious effort is required to placate the ghosts … food, such as noodle mountains and decorated fruits, is displayed in magnificent if gaudy ceremony.**

name sounds like 'rising in status every year'. Increasingly rare, though, are the bird's nest and barley cakes, still prepared to ancient recipes at the **Chan Yee Jai** cake shop, established in the 1920s (*199 Queen's Rd, Central, Sheung Wan; ✆ 2453 8414;* Ⓜ *MTR Sheung Wan Station Exit A2; open: daily 0900–1900; no credit cards accepted*).

The New Year is a perfect time to **marry** and once again food plays a key role. The bridegroom presents his new in-laws with *ka nui beng* to bless the marriage: sweet cakes such as those prepared by the **Kee Wah** cake shop (*see page 75*). The bride will toast each guest with tea and, in return, receive gifts and lucky money, *lycee*, in red packets. And the wedding feast itself may still comprise a basin meal, *pan choi*: a traditional Hakka dish known colloquially as 'many treasures in a wooden bowl'. Eight layers of different foods are served to groups of eight diners, who all gleefully attack the central bowl with their chopsticks. Basin meals are still served at **Kam Tin** (*87 Pat Heung Sheung Tsuen, Yuen Long, New Territories; ✆ 2488 3417;* Ⓜ *bus 54 from Yuen Long station, bus 65K from Tai Po Market station, bus 251M from Tsing Yi MTR station; open: daily 1200–2100 or later; reservations recommended, no credit cards accepted;* ❺). The noise, mêlée and sheer enjoyment factor is the very essence of celebration!

Food etiquette and culture

If there is one golden rule in Chinese dining, it is that **food is to be enjoyed**; nothing, but nothing, must get in its way! If your table ends up resembling a minor battlefield, with spillage, crumpled napkins and the plate almost (but not quite) empty, then you should be congratulated on a job well done. Yet beyond the noise and the gusto, there are subtle, behavioural nuances and customs that the respectful visitor will wish to honour.

ORDERING

When selecting Chinese dishes, a good rule of thumb is to order one dish per person with one extra – but then dishes are always placed centrally, to share. Meals are inevitably best when there are enough of you to order several dishes, and the connoisseur will aim to combine all the five tastes of Chinese cooking in a single meal (sweet, salty, hot, bitter and acidic) so as to achieve a harmonious balance of *Ying* (negative influences) and *Yang* (positive influences). Similarly, a balance is sought between the textures: crunchy and tender, dry and moist – *Ying* and *Yang* aside, this is actually quite sensible if you think about it. If there are only two of you, you might be better off ordering, say, one meat, one vegetable and one rice or noodle-based dish.

CHOPSTICKS

When you are resting your chopsticks during a meal, place them flat on the bowl or chopstick rest – not sticking up out of your food as this is considered unlucky, in the same way that turning over a whole fish is just not done, as that would be symbolic of a capsizing fishing boat. It is considered impolite to take food from a communal dish and eat it straight away; instead, bring the food to your own bowl or dish first, even if only to pause briefly. It is, however, perfectly acceptable – even polite – to take a choice morsel from a central dish and place it in your neighbour or guest's bowl! If you are unfamiliar with using chopsticks, try thinking of the lower chopstick as the anvil: rest it in the crook between your thumb and hand, rather like a pen, but hold it more firmly by using the tip of your ring finger to apply gentle pressure. Then manoeuvre the upper chopstick by using the tips of your thumb, forefinger and middle finger.

RICE

Rice is normally served in separate bowls. It is normal to use a little rice in your bowl as a bed on which to rest the food you take, in small quantities at a time, from the central dishes, and to eat the rice towards the end of the meal. You should feel perfectly at home using your chopsticks to shovel rice into your mouth, raising your bowl to your lips! Rice serves to balance the meal, to ensure that you have feasted well enough; it is therefore polite to empty your own individual bowl, whereas it sends a complimentary message to your host if a little rice in the shared dishes remains uneaten, as a symbol of the generosity of the meal.

TEA

Tea will automatically accompany your meal without cost in most Chinese restaurants, and is drunk without milk, lemon or sugar. Bear in mind that it is considered very rude to fill your own cup without first filling all others at the table. If you are dining with locals, you'll find that they normally simply tap the table three times with their middle finger to signify their thanks. When a teapot is empty, simply leave the lid slightly open, or turn the lid upside down, and the brew should be magically replenished.

SERVICE

Don't be put off if you get what appears to be quite cursory, even rude, service; food is a serious business, and it just isn't part of the culture to waste too much time on niceties.

TIPPING

Tipping is normally expected – but not outrageously so. In restaurants, a 10 per cent service charge is usually added to the bill and, whether paying by credit card or with cash, it is the norm to round up the bill or leave a few coins or small notes as a token gesture. Drinks bought at a bar do not normally command a tip but if drinks are brought to your table, then again, a token gesture would be appreciated.

SMOKING

Hong Kong still smokes quite heavily and, apart from the more expensive restaurants, very few establishments have non-smoking sections.

Menu decoder

abalone – shellfish also known as sea ear (the shell is a source of mother-of-pearl) prized for its tender yet rubbery texture rather than its (fairly bland) taste

baak faan – plain steamed rice

beggar's chicken – originally a Peking dish of a chicken stuffed with vegetables, herbs and onions, wrapped in lotus leaves and then sealed in clay before baking slowly; also called fortune chicken

belachan – fermented prawn paste, used as a condiment in Chinese cooking

bird's nest soup – *yin wo*: made from brewing nests of swifts or small swallows, prized for the glutinous secretions from the birds' salivary glands

bok choi – also *pak choi*; Chinese cabbage with long white stalks and dark green leaves

cai – generic term to refer to meat, vegetables and fish; one half of a meal, accompanied by *faan*

cep – a type of mushroom

cha – tea

char kway teow – a Chinese dish of broad rice noodles, with sweet sauce, bean sprouts, Chinese sausage or fish cake

char siu, char siu bau – sweetish barbecued pork, fluffy steamed bun (*dim sum*), filled with diced barbecued pork

char siu cheung faan – steamed rice roll filled with barbecued pork (*dim sum*)

chau faan – fried rice

chau sin wu – fried shredded eel, normally served with plain rice

chendol – an Asian jelly dessert made from red kidney beans, coconut milk and brown sugar

cheng ting – Chinese dessert: syrup with herbal jelly, barley and dates

cheung yun – Chinese spring rolls

choi sum – a Chinese green vegetable, with little yellow flowers, usually served with oyster sauce

chung yau beng – Peking fried onion cakes

cloud ear fungus – a brown/black mushroom, normally sold dried, which takes on a jelly-like yet crunchy texture

congee – a Chinese porridge, made from rice cooked slowly over a low heat for several hours, served with a range of fish, meat or vegetables

daikon – large white radish, popular in Chinese (*loh buk*) and Japanese cuisine

dai pai dong – technically an open-air Chinese restaurant, although now used for basic restaurants which offer traditional street-stall fare

dao see – fermented, salted black beans

dau fu – tofu or beancurd, a jellified cake of soya bean and water

dhosa – light, crispy Indian pancake filled with spicy potatoes and onions dim sum – sweet and savoury buns, dumplings and mini dishes, served for breakfast and lunch

di wang – a leafy Asian vegetable

drunken chicken – *jui gai*, a Shanghai dish where the chicken is marinated before cooking in Shaoxing wine

drunken prawns – a delicacy where live prawns are placed in Chinese wine and later boiled

enokitake – golden mushrooms, with tiny cream-coloured caps and tall, thin stems

es delima – Malaysian dessert, made from water chestnuts in sago and coconut milk

faan – generally used to refer to rice, though also covers noodles, bread and all cereals served as basic accompaniments to *cai*

fish balls – minced squid, shrimp and/or fish, reconstituted into balls, normally served in noodle soups or *congee* (rice gruel)

fish maw – a delicacy: part of the fish stomach

fish sauce – pungent brown sauce made from salted dried fish

five spice – powders of star anise, brown peppercorns, fennel, cinnamon and cloves

gado gado – cold Indonesian/Malay 'salad' of bean sprouts, potato, bean curd and rice cakes topped with spicy peanut sauce and rice crackers

gai bau – steamed chicken dumpling (*dim sum*)

gai haw bai toey – Thai fried chicken in *pandanas* leaves

gai tom kla – Thai chicken and coconut soup

garam masala – a sweet, mild Indian curry mix, including coriander, cumin, black cardamom and cloves

garoupa – a white fish, prolific in southeast Asia

geung – ginger: Canton ginger is said to be the most aromatic

glutinous rice – a 'sticky rice' with a high starch content, commonly used for desserts

gong chau ngau – Beijing dish of beef strips dry-fried with chilli, eaten with bread pockets

gong biao chi ding – Classic Szechuan dish of fried chicken, green peppers and peanuts

gooi – Korean tabletop barbecue with meat or fish and vegetables

ha gau – steamed shrimp dumpling (*dim sum*)

ho yip faan – glutinous rice wrapped in lotus leaves

hoi sin sauce – thick brown sauce made from soya beans

hokkien mee – Chinese dish of yellow noodles, fried with

▲ Thai beef salad

meat and seafood and topped
with strips of yellow omelette

ji ma ha – sesame prawn on toast
(*dim sum*)

jiu – distilled Chinese rice wine,
with a strong, dry taste

kaen cud – Thai soup

kaen pad – Thai curry

kai tom kha – Thai lemongrass
chicken soup with coconut milk

kang kong – Chinese spinach with
a thick stem

khao phad – Thai fried rice

khao suai – Thai white rice

kobe beef – the best quality beef
with marbled texture, from
cattle fed only on milk

kung – Thai prawns

kway teo – Thai broad noodles

larb – a Thai dish of minced pork
or chicken, with herbs and
spices, eaten wrapped in
lettuce leaves

lo chau – dark soy sauce,
normally used to lend a dark
colour to braised or slow-
cooked dishes and sauces

loh baak gau – turnip cakes

lotus – the root of the lotus plant
(much cited in literature and
rife with symbolism!) is used
as a vegetable; the seed pods
are used in medicines and the
seeds are sometimes boiled

whole in tonic soups, and often puréed to make sweets or cake fillings

mai daang – the bill

miu gwai cha – rosebud tea

monosodium glutamate (MSG) – a widely used condiment used for its saltiness and translucent thickening qualities (*mei jing*)

nasi goreng – Malay or Indonesian rice dish with chicken or beef, topped with strips of egg

nasi padang – generic term which refers to Malay or Indonesian rice-based dishes, usually served with meat and vegetables

oyster sauce – a thick brown sauce made from oysters, dark soy sauce and salt, used as much for its colouring as its fish flavouring

Peking duck – slowly roasted whole duck, repeatedly basted with honey, served in three courses (skin and meat, both eaten wrapped in wheat pancakes with spring onion and cucumber, and broth)

rendang – Malay or Indonesian beef stew like a mild curry, made with coconut milk and spices

sang chau or see yau – light soy sauce; the best grade of soy, with a delicate and fine flavour, normally used for the final seasoning, and in stir-fried and steamed dishes

satay or sate – skewers of meat (chicken or beef but not usually pork, as Malay food generally observes Muslim etiquette) or fish, barbecued and served a mildly spicy peanut sauce

see lo chau or sang chau – soy

se gang – Snake soup

shabu shabu – Japanese one-pot (*nabemono*) or 'steamboat' meal

shark's fin soup – variously, *woon jai chi* or *yiu chi gang*; the fin is normally sold dried, and then resoaked for many hours, to produce a slightly gelatinous texture

shitake – Japanese or Chinese brown mushrooms, with a firm, meaty flavour

siu long bau – Shanghai dumpling with minced pork, steamed in a bamboo case

siu mai – crab, pork and prawn dumpling (*dim sum*)

straw mushroom – a tall, thin, leafy mushroom also known as paddy straw mushroom

taro – a root vegetable similar to sweet potato, with spinach-like leaves and asparagus-like stalks

tau hui – a soya bean by-product, served as a local dessert with sugar syrup

tom yum kum – Thai hot and sour seafood soup

wonton – Chinese dumpling: a thin flour wrapper filled with minced meat and/or shrimp, often served with noodle soups

woo gok – deep-fried *taro* dumpling (*dim sum*)

yi fu – noodle

yiu char gwai – deep-fried Chinese 'breadsticks', often sold at street stalls, eaten with *congee*

yiu jiu – roast suckling pig

yum cha – literally 'drink tea', this is synonymous with a hot meal (breakfast, brunch or lunch) with *dim sum*

Recipes

Cantonese steamed whole fish

Steaming – widely used in Chinese cooking – is ideal for fish as it preserves the texture and subtle aromas; for this recipe sea bass or snapper would be best, but any white fleshed fish with a firm texture will do. Simple boiled rice is a good accompaniment.

Serves 6

INGREDIENTS

1 fish (700g)
1 large carrot
3 spring onions
8 slices fresh ginger
4–6 Chinese dried black mushrooms, soaked in water, then drained and squeezed dry
2 tbsp vegetable oil
2 tbsp light soy sauce
1½ tbsp rice wine or dry sherry
½ tsp sugar
fresh coriander

If possible, ask your fishmonger to gut and scale the fish; rinse and wipe the fish dry with kitchen towel. Make four to five diagonal cuts through the flesh on each side, to allow the flavours to penetrate. Place the fish on a slightly oiled plate that fits in your steamer. In a small bowl, mix the soy sauce, rice wine and sugar, and pour over the fish. Shred the carrot, spring onions, mushrooms and ginger finely, and arrange them over the fish.

Add just a little water to the steamer (it is important that when the water boils it does not come into contact with the fish). Place the fish in the steamer, cover and steam gently for 25 to 30 minutes. To test whether the fish is cooked, use a flat knife: the flesh should lift easily off the bone.

Carefully remove the dish from the steamer, retaining all the juices. Sprinkle with coriander leaves and serve immediately.

Peking crispy shredded beef with chillies, in sesame bread pockets

You can vary the amount of chilli in this typical northern Chinese recipe according to taste. Its success lies in its freshness and crispiness, and so should be served immediately and only cooked once the bread is ready and piping hot. The sesame bread pockets can be mostly prepared in advance and the final baking saved till the end. The filled pockets are eaten with fingers. To complete the meal, serve with a fresh vegetable dish, such as lightly steamed broccoli florets with a black bean dipping sauce.

Sesame bread (makes 12 pockets)

INGREDIENTS

625g plain flour
75ml vegetable oil (preferably ground nut oil)
300ml boiling water
2 tsp salt
2 tbsp white sesame seeds

Heat the vegetable oil in a saucepan and stir in 125g of flour, stirring constantly until the mix turns a light golden colour. Remove from the heat and leave to cool.

In a large bowl, mix the remaining flour with the boiling water quickly. Cover the bowl and set aside for 5 minutes.

Sprinkle a little oil on a cool, flat surface and knead the dough for about seven minutes until it is smooth and pliable. Divide it into 12 pieces. To create pockets, roll each piece into a square, and spread a little of the flour and oil mixture on one side only and season with salt. Next fold the square into two, and pinch the edges to seal in the paste. Roll again to make the pocket a little larger, and with a kitchen brush dampen one side and sprinkle over the sesame seeds.

Heat the oven to Gas Mark 7 (200°C/ 400°F). When it is time to bake the bread pockets, place them on an oiled baking tray and bake for 5 minutes on one side, turn and bake for 5 minutes on the other side, until crisp and slightly puffed up.

Crispy shredded beef with chillies

Serves 6

INGREDIENTS

500g rump beef

75ml light soy sauce

1 tbsp rice wine, *sake* or dry sherry

1 tsp sugar

3 tbsp vegetable oil (preferably ground nut oil)

2 fresh chillies, finely chopped

sesame oil

1 tbsp finely chopped ginger

Cut the beef into fine strips, 1cm wide. Place in a large bowl, add the rice wine, ginger,

chillies, soy sauce, 1 tbsp vegetable oil, salt and pepper. Stir, cover and leave to marinate for 2 hours.

Later add the remaining 2 tbsp oil to a wok and heat until the oil smokes; add the meat and rapidly stir-fry over a high heat for a few minutes, until the meat is crisped at the edges. Finally, add a dash of sesame oil, and salt and pepper to taste.

Serve the meat immediately on a large dish, and allow your guests to break open and fill their own sesame bread pockets.

▲ Steamed fish with spring onion

Published by Thomas Cook Publishing
Thomas Cook Holdings Ltd
PO Box 227
Thorpe Wood
Peterborough PE3 6PU
United Kingdom

Telephone: 01733 503571
Email: books@thomascook.com

Text © 2001 Thomas Cook Publishing
Maps © 2001 Thomas Cook Publishing

ISBN 1 841570 88 5

Distributed in the United States of
America by the Globe Pequot Press,
PO Box 480, Guilford, Connecticut
06437, USA

Publisher: Donald Greig
Commissioning Editor: Deborah Parker
Map Editor: Bernard Horton

Project management: Dial House
    Publishing
Series Editor: Christopher Catling
Copy Editor: Lucy Thomson
Proofreader: Kate Owen

Series and cover design: WhiteLight
Cover artwork: WhiteLight and
    Kaarin Wall
Text layout: SJM Design Consultancy,
    Dial House Publishing
Maps prepared by Polly Senior
    Cartography

Repro and image setting: PDQ Digital
    Media Solutions Ltd
Printed and bound in Italy by
    Eurografica SpA

Written and researched by: **Taryn Nixon**
    and **Odile Bourras-Laspelades**

The photographer would like to thank the
following places: Arirang Mongolian
Barbecue, Dicken's Bar, The Grand Hyatt
Hotel, Joe Bananas, Kublai's Mongolian
Fresh Grilled, Lai Ching Heen Restaurant,
Man Wah, The Peak Café, Peking Garden,
The Peninsula and Super Star Seafood
Restaurant.

The authors would like to thank all their
'gourmand' friends in Hong Kong for their
nuggets of information and help,
especially Chris Strachan and Peggy Wu.

We would like to thank Ethel Davies for
the photographs used in this book, to
whom the copyright belongs.